Y0-BZK-142

PSYCHIC BEAM
TO BEYOND

by Peter and Jane Boulton

THROUGH THE PSYCHIC SENSITIVE,

Lenora Huett

with love,

Jane Boulton

DeVorss & Company
Box 550, Marina del Rey, California 90291

Copyright © 1983
by Jane Boulton

All Rights Reserved

ISBN: 0-87516-514-1
Library of Congress Card Catalog Number: 82-074522

Printed in the United States of America

Contents

consciousness . . . identity . . . free will . . . individuals merging . . . energy force . . . entities . . .
Mind . . . soul groups . . . reincarnation . . . levels of existence . . . space beings . . . spheres . . .
3,4,5 dimensions . . . personal information . . .
Atlanteans . . . birth contract . . . karmic debts
. . . earth lessons . . . love/hate . . . Mozart . . .
planet lives . . . spiritual development of countries
. . . soul entering body . . . life tasks . . . suicide
. . . abortion . . . objective/subjective existence . . .
soul groups . . . karma groups . . . motivation for
entities born on earth . . . slate not wiped clean
. . . planet lives . . . soul growth measurement . . .
self-conscious life forms . . . animal souls.

Preface

Jane Boulton

Thanks to the inspired research of Gina Cerminara, author of *Many Mansions*, who gave us a special list of psychic sensitives, we were led to visit some of them. And what a flood of revelation followed!

Although our intention was one of purely personal illumination, it seems all too dazzling to hoard.

The material of this book came through the fine psychic sensitive, Lenora Huett, who proved the clearest for the purposes of this work. Practical, warm and cheerful, Lenora is as down-to-earth as a kindly country neighbor. Her concerns for her husband and children, an orderly house and a deeply religious life show in the qualities of goodness and humility that shine through her.

For years she had been interested in and exposed to various psychic phenomena. Then she started a meditation group experience and was led to try automatic writing until she found herself gradually transmitting messages from those on the other side. As she pursued this, she discovered that her skill and clarity of reception increased with practice. She also found that she could be helpful to people with their questions and problems.

Unlike some psychics, Lenora does not do a "reading" on a person, as such, nor does she volunteer information; she works only from questions brought to her. For this reason, Peter, my husband, compiled a long series of complex questions for what she calls her "source."

She does not pretend to know how the communication works. "This state of mind is not like a trance," she said, for she is aware of the messages that come through her. Scientists, developing new methods of testing, relate the vibratory levels to Alpa, Beta and deeper levels, while she describes it as "being in neutral" and laughs that she may forget to take it out of neutral after the session.

All material that follows was carefully preserved on tape, then typed. Two sessions, by telephone, were also taped. In them one can hear the voice difference between what she is repeating from the "source" and what she is interpreting from symbols and pictures.

We wish a sample cassette could be provided with the book to allow readers to hear for themselves the changes in communication levels.

In the midst of the taping, Peter asked her "source:" "Is there a constructive purpose in our communicating through Mrs. Huett at this time?"

The answer came: "IT'S HELPFUL TO THE END THAT WHEN AN IDEA NEEDS TO BE SEEDED, IT CAN BE GIVEN TO THOSE WHO WILL ACT UPON IT OR USE IT IN A HELPFUL MANNER FOR MANKIND."

For this reason I have persevered to get this work published, and all quotes from the "source" will be in all caps.

Considering the abstract nature of the material and its density, we cannot expect a sudden grasp of its teachings. One reading will not suffice to absorb the range, for this is a book to be studied. Profound, religious, inspiring, it concerns the knowledge of life.

After reading the finished manuscript, Lenora commented: "I recall that each time we did this, there was such a feeling of awe about the situation."

That perfectly describes our own emotions of reverence for the rare and remarkable experience we hope you will share of being in the presence of a Master.

PSYCHIC BEAM TO BEYOND

"When we absorb spiritual knowledge in its true meaning, something works within our souls like a spiritual Sun. Spiritual knowledge is a bond of union between men. We do not promulgate human brotherhood by means of programmes, but we lay the foundations of brotherhood whenever similar ideals are kindled in a number of human beings, whenever others look up as we ourselves do to what we hold sacred."
—Rudolf Steiner
from *Macrocosm and Microcosm*

"Infinite progression is concrete being."
—Mary Baker Eddy

CHAPTER 1

Present Earth
Conditions

It was a fresh, bright morning in November when my husband and I drove up to Lenora Huett's home in San Jose, California. A plump, pleasant woman, her face beamed a warm welcome even as she settled down breathlessly from the rush of seeing her children off to school and getting her house into apple pie order. There were just the three of us, Lenora, Peter and I, all anxious to contact what she calls her "source."

Gina Cerminara had given us Lenora's name as a notable psychic sensitive, and from the number of telephone calls and scheduled appointments, she had obviously been discovered by many others. To keep up with the demands of a family, a household, and her ties with the public, this woman had to be super organized, and she was. The pressures did not disturb her own good disposition, but her husband, a contractor, grew very impatient about the number of people interrupting their family life and regretted her involvement in this field.

Lenora invited us to join her at the diningroom table where she had at her place a blank piece of paper and a ballpoint pen. For this pre-arranged appointment, Peter had

1

brought along his tape recorder which she assured him was fine with her. Peter made a trial run with the tape cassette, announcing the date and the persons involved, to be sure it was recording properly.

"I hope you'll excuse any telephone interruptions," she said. "With so many people calling, my life is not my own."

Peter smiled and convinced her we had plenty of time and she was not to feel worried by that. A businessman/entrepreneur, he was a great believer in the importance of doing one's homework, and had spent many nights compiling his list of questions.

"Let's start with a definition," he said.

Closing her eyes for a moment, Lenora took a deep breath and picked up her pen. We were all expectant.

"Ask your Source to define life," Peter started.

Lenora was looking down at the paper as her pen made a series of large loops as though she were practicing penmanship. Instantly the message came. Not on the paper, but spoken clearly and firmly at a most surprising speed.

"LIFE IS ONGOINGNESS. LIFE IS ALL THINGS. LIFE IS. LIFE IS NOT JUST HUMAN-NESS AS MAN CONCEIVES IT TO BE. LIFE IS THE VERY ENERGY THAT IS AROUND ALL THINGS AND IN ALL THINGS, EVEN RECEIVED IN INANIMATE OBJECTS THAT MAN CAN VIEW WITH HIS PHYSICAL EYE."

Her voice as we knew it had not changed, but the pace of her words had quickened as though she were reading a text. Then her eyes looked up at us with a preoccupied expression as though she were still straining to listen. Once again the words were slow. "I just get 'LIFE IS' and it seems to spring like that and stop."

"Great!" said my husband enthusiastically. "What are the clearest signs of human progress?"

"FIRST, THE MEASURE OF PEACE THAT COMES UPON THE EARTH, THE MEASURE OF CONCERN FOR OTHERS WITHIN THE

FRAMEWORK OF THE WORLD, THE HEALTH STANDARDS—NOT ALONE THOSE OF THE PHYSICAL AREA, BUT THOSE ALSO OF MENTAL HEALTH. PEACE."

PB Are there any specific suggestions that could be made to aid world progress?

S   LISTEN, LISTEN, LISTEN. LISTEN TO THOSE THINGS WHICH ARE BEING SAID WITHIN THE WORLD FRAMEWORK. LISTEN TO THE CRIES OF NEED. LISTEN TO WHAT YOUR FELLOW MAN IS ACTUALLY SAYING. HELP TO MANIFEST ROOTS THAT ARE INTERESTED IN THE DEVELOPMENT OF THEIR OWN UNDERSTANDING. LISTEN CLOSELY TO THOSE WHO ARE IN POWER AND JUDGE THEIR WORTH. DO NOT WITHDRAW FROM THE WORLD, BUT ENTER INTO A GREATER INTEREST IN THE OVERALL PLAN.

PB By saying "listen" you are speaking in the larger sense? You don't mean just listen to the words that are coming from our leaders?

S   RIGHT.

PB How best may one work for peace?

S   THIS IS A MATTER THAT HAS TO BE CONSIDERED VERY DEEPLY. IT IS SOMETHING THAT IS NOT FORTHCOMING IN THE NEXT FEW YEARS. THERE ARE MANY PIECES OF GROUNDWORK BEING LAID EVEN AT THIS TIME. IT IS MOST ESSENTIAL THAT MAN FIND PEACE WITHIN HIMSELF AND THOSE RELATED TO HIM IN ANY WAY, FOR ONLY THROUGH THIS WILL MAN MORE THOROUGHLY BE ABLE TO COPE WITH OUTER PROBLEMS. AND AS HE DOES WITHIN, HE WILL BE ABLE TO DO WITHOUT.

THOSE THINGS THAT ARE DONE ON A SMALLER SCALE CAN THEN BE DONE ON A LARGER SCALE: FOR, AS MAN CAN UNDERSTAND HIMSELF, HE WILL THEN BE BETTER ABLE TO UNDERSTAND HIS NATION, AND IN TURN HIS NATION WILL BE BETTER ABLE TO UNDERSTAND OTHER AREAS OF THE WORLD, AND SO ON OUT INTO THE UNIVERSE.

PB   Is it better to work alone or to have a tiny influence in an organization going in a better direction than another organization?

(The answer came strongly.)

S   IT IS NECESSARY TO WORK WITHIN THE STRUCTURE OF AN ORGANIZATION, FOR ONLY THROUGH THIS CAN POWER BE GIVEN TO THOSE IDEAS WHICH ARE YOURS. AND YET, IT IS ALSO NECESSARY THAT YOU WORK CONSTANTLY IN THE ALONENESS THAT IS AROUND YOU.

(Now the words came slowly again in her own conversational manner.)

LH   I just get "IN THE ALONENESS THAT IS AROUND YOU" and then it stops.

PB   That's fine. Let's go on.
     By organization, are you thinking of national or state governmental organizations, or private?

S   MANY OF THE ORGANIZATIONS WHICH GO UNDER THE FRONT OF A PEACE MOVEMENT ARE NOT NECESSARILY SO. AND IT IS NECESSARY TO INVESTIGATE THOROUGHLY THE PURPOSES AND PRINCIPLES BEHIND EACH OF THESE GROUPS BEFORE YOU ASSOCIATE YOURSELF WITH THEM. IT IS ALSO WELL TO NOTE THAT MANY THINGS WITHIN GOVERNMENT ARE NOT WHAT THEY ARE SUPPOSED TO BE.

PB   There are many who say we are not responsible for those others about us.

(Immediately the reading voice became alive and brisk.)

S   THIS IS TRUE. YOU ARE NOT TOTALLY RESPONSIBLE. HOWEVER, IT IS YOUR RESPONSIBILITY TO PLACE ALL THINGS WITHIN THEIR PATH THAT WILL BE OF BENEFIT TO THEM. IT IS NOT FOR YOU TO JUDGE THAT WHICH WOULD BE RIGHT OR WRONG FOR THEM.

PB Does this mean that each entity influences those that he comes in contact with?

S TO SOME EXTENT. TO SOME DEGREE, YES. THERE IS ALWAYS THAT INFLUENCE WHICH WOULD RUB OFF. MANY TIMES IT IS AN UNSEEN OR UNSPOKEN EFFECT, EVEN AS THE JOINING OF AURAS, WHICH CAN BENEFIT THOSE WITHOUT A KNOWING OF ACCOMPLISHMENT.

PB Ask your Source to explain about the joining of auras.

S THIS IS WHEN TWO PEOPLE COME IN CONTACT WITH EACH OTHER AND THE AURA OR THE AURIC FIELD ABOUT A PERSON, WHICH IS FULL OF ENERGY AND LIGHT AND VIBRATIONS, CAN THEN BE INTERCHANGEABLY MIXED WITH THAT ONE WHO IS CLOSE. IT IS A MELTING OF ENERGIES SO THAT EACH ONE CAN DRAW FROM THE OTHER. IT IS NECESSARILY BENEFICIAL TO THE LESSER ONE. IT IS NOT ALWAYS BENEFICIAL TO THE HIGHER ONE. THERE ARE TIMES WHEN THIS CAN DRAW STRENGTH FROM ONE AND NOT BE REPLENISHED BY THE OTHER, DEPENDING ON THAT WHICH IS ABOUT THE PERSON.

(I found myself intrigued with the use of language that was so different from our contemporary speech. Who *was* this being in contact with us? Peter seemed to treat it as a perfectly normal communication, and of course, Lenora was doing what she did every day, but I was amazed.)

PB Since each entity has his own lessons to learn, isn't it the obligation of others not to interfere with his free will?

S HOW COULD YOU INTERFERE WITH HIS FREE WILL? YOU CAN ONLY INFLUENCE OR SHOW. YOU MAY NOT FORCE YOUR WILL UPON THAT ONE, TRUE, BUT IT IS NOT AN INTERFERENCE OF THEIR FREE WILL IF YOU EXPOSE THEM TO THAT WHICH IS RIGHT AND GOOD. REMEMBER, THAT WHICH IS RIGHT AND GOOD FOR YOU MAY NOT NECESSARILY BE THAT WHICH THEY ARE SEEKING. BUT YOU MUST MAKE THE ENDEAVOR TO EXPOSE THEM TO IT.

PB Why do there seem to be so many who are deliberately trying to influence and guide others?

S   THEY HAVE YET MANY OF THEIR OWN LESSONS TO LEARN. THEY ARE TRYING TO FEEL THE ALL POWER WITHIN THEMSELVES. THEY ARE TRYING TO FORCE THEIR WAY, AND THIS IS THE VERY THING THAT THEY FIGHT AGAINST WITHIN THEMSELVES. AND YET, THEY ARE TRYING TO DO IT TO THE OUTSIDE ENTITIES. IT GIVES THEM A FALSE SENSE OF SECURITY AND A FALSE SENSE OF POWER.

PB Mankind's opinion of scientific research seems very retarding. How can this hold-back attitude be overcome?

S   THIS AGE THAT IS NOW PRESENT WITH MAN WILL OVERCOME MUCH OF THIS, FOR THOSE WHO ARE IN BOTH AREAS OF SCIENTIFIC RESEARCH AND OF PHILOSOPHICAL UNDERSTANDING WILL BE MEETING WITH EACH OTHER IN THE UNDERSTANDING THAT MANY OF THE PHRASES AND ATTITUDES WHICH HAVE BEEN USED ARE SAYING THE SAME THINGS, ARE OF SIMILAR NATURE, ARE BACKING EACH OTHER IN KNOWLEDGE.

   THE APPEARANCE OF MANY OF THE ADVANCEMENTS THAT COME WILL SEEM RETROGRESSION TO THE OUTER EYE. HOWEVER, KNOW THAT PROGRESS IS BEING MADE ON ALL LEVELS AND ALL PLACES AT THIS TIME.

   THERE IS MUCH THAT APPEARS TO IMPAIR THE GROWTH OF PEACE. AND YET, BE IT KNOWN THAT PEACE GROUNDWORK IS BEING LAID.

PB Is the help that comes from studying the past somewhat overrated?

S   ONLY IN THAT MAN HAS NOT YET LEARNED HIS LESSON. HE IS YET TO MAKE THE SAME MISTAKES OVER AND OVER. IT IS TRUE THAT MUCH THAT HAS COME BEFORE WILL BE REPEATED, BUT THIS IS ONLY BECAUSE OF THE FOLLY OF MAN, HIS LACK OF LEARNING.

PB   What is maturity?

S   THIS IS THE OVERALL PICTURE THAT ONE CAN TAKE TO
     HIMSELF IN ALL TRUTH. IT IS THE BEGINNING TO REALIZE
     THE LACK OF CONFIDENCE AND KNOWLEDGE AND TO REALIZE
     THE LACK IN MANY AREAS. THIS IS NOT TO BERATE HIMSELF
     BECAUSE OF IT, BUT IT IS THE INNER KNOWLEDGE THAT ALL
     THINGS ARE EVER-INCREASING, AND AS ONE INCREASES WITH
     AGE HE CAN INCREASE WITH MATURITY, THOUGH NOT NECES-
     SARILY. ONE IS NOT DEPENDENT UPON THE OTHER. IT IS THE
     KNOWING WITHIN SO THAT ONE CAN SEE A BROADER SENSE, A
     GREATER EMPATHY OF ONE'S FELLOW BEINGS AND ALSO THE
     CONDITIONS WHICH SURROUND THAT PARTICULAR ENTITY. IT
     IS A DETACHMENT OF THOUGHT WITHOUT A DETACHMENT OF
     SELF.

(Lenora had put down her pen. After the first tunnel of
loops she had made at the beginning, there were no more
marks on the paper. We were later to learn this meant communications were flowing well. In future sessions we would
see her make the same circles when she wasn't getting a message clearly or couldn't understand. Evidently this writing
was the handle for staying in contact.)

PB   It is said one should love one's country. If one . . .
(And just as he said that the telephone rang. Lenora, looking
grieved, went quickly to the kitchen to answer it and Peter
turned off his tape machine. I wondered if we would be able
to continue our communication after she had been brought
out of her other level. We could hear her speaking kindly to
someone who wanted an appointment with her. Once that
was arranged, she hurried back, all apologies.)

LH   Oh, I'm so sorry. I know this is very important informa-
     tion for you. Now, where were we?

PB   I'll start my question again.
     It is said one should love one's country. If one faces a

circumstance where the governing body is wrong, then some say it is the obligation of the citizen to obey anyway. Others say the citizen should fight the system. And others believe the more responsible citizens should go into exile so they may be available to help when the bad government fails. How does an entity know what to do, what is right?

S   IT IS A MOST DIFFICULT QUESTION YOU POSE, FOR THE ANSWER IS NOT ONE THAT CAN COME READILY NOR COVER AND ENCOMPASS ALL TIME OR SPACE. THE SOUL THAT HAS PASSED BEYOND THE LIMITATIONS OF EARTH AND WORLD IS HARD PUT TO COMMENT ON SOMETHING SUCH AS THIS. HOWEVER, THE SOUL MUST DO THAT WHICH APPEARS TO BE RIGHT, THAT WITH WHICH HE CAN LIVE WITHIN HIS OWN CONSCIOUS STATE. IT IS NECESSARY THAT ONE NOT DESERT THE SINKING SHIP BUT STAY THERE. THERE WILL BE MANY BATTLES LOST, MANY PEOPLE RUN OVER.

(Lenora stopped to explain what she saw)
LH It looks like a piece of road equipment flattening them out into the asphalt.

S   MANY PERSONS WILL BE RUN OVER BEFORE THAT WHICH IS RIGHT CAN COME ABOUT. HOWEVER, ONE MUST NEVER STOP ASSERTING HIS OWN POLITICAL BELIEFS OR RIGHTS. CONTINUE TO VOTE. CONTINUE TO WORK FOR THAT WHICH SEEMS TO BE RIGHT. YOU FEEL AS THOUGH YOU ARE ONE SMALL LIGHT GLEAMING IN THE DARKNESS; HOWEVER IT DOES NOT DISPEL THAT BIT OF DARKNESS WHICH IS AROUND YOU. CONTINUE TO REMAIN TRUE TO THAT WHICH YOU BELIEVE.

PB Is the Unites States election . . .
Once again the phone rang and Lenora left the room. Peter turned off the tape recorder and looked at me. "It seems to be coming through well," he said, smiling. "Do you think this tires her?" I asked. By way of answer, he said: "Just a few more questions in this session and then we'll stop. There is so much ground to cover."

When Lenora returned to the room he asked if she felt up to a few more questions and she seemed relieved that we were almost at an end. As willing and as interested as she was, there is no doubt that this means of communications uses up energies of the psychic sensitives, as we were to learn in time to come.

"Go ahead with the last questions," Lenora urged.

PB Is the United States election system so structured that Universal Mind can guide and even control the election outcome?

S Not always. There are many loopholes which even universal mind cannot fathom. These take the very devious directions that man has devised and in time the ultimate result is one that is good. Bear with it. Do not feel that even though these loopholes present great problems at this time, they cannot be overcome. Time is a factor which is important.

PB Define time.

S Time is a very indefinable object or word, as the case may be, for time in itself is relative, even though it is blocked off in a matter of days or weeks or months. The seeming slowness or speed of it is relative to the immediate emotional response that comes from a person. For example, if a person feels joy, time seems to stand still, while for a similar person experiencing pain for the same amount of time, it is unending. Time is the essence of eternity.

PB Is this American election system of government more reliable than having individual kings or princes or potentates?

S Yes, by far.

PB Will there always be conflict against man in his earth form?

LH It says, No.

S   No. THERE WILL COME A TIME UPON THE EARTH WHEN
    MANY THINGS HAVE BEEN SMOOTHED AWAY AND MAN WILL
    THEN BE ABLE TO MAKE MORE RAPID PROGRESS IN THOSE
    THINGS WHICH TRULY COUNT. INSTEAD OF FIGHTING HIM-
    SELF AND FELLOW MAN, HE WILL THEN BE FIGHTING FOR THE
    GOOD AND THE RIGHT. AND BY FIGHTING, WE DO NOT MEAN
    PERSONAL CONFLICT OR CONFLICT WITH SWORDS, BUT CON-
    FLICT WITH NATURE AND THE FORCES ABOUT HIM. HE WILL
    BETTER LEARN TO UTILIZE THE FORCES WHICH CAN ACCOM-
    PLISH GREAT THINGS. THEN HE WILL LEAVE HIS EARTH
    PLANE, BUT NOT IN A SPIRITUAL FORM. HE LEAVES IT IN A
    PHYSICAL FORM AND FINDS THAT HE CANNOT CONQUER BUT
    CULTIVATE SPACE.

(As a pacifist, I could not, at this point, resist asking a
a question of my own:)

JB Has every entity killed and been killed?

S   NEARLY ALL. THERE ARE A FEW VERY RARE SOULS UPON THE
    EARTH WHO HAVE COME IN WITH A GREAT DEAL OF PURITY
    AND HAVE REMAINED THAT WAY THROUGH THEIR MANY
    LIFETIMES. THIS IS EXTREMELY UNUSUAL. YOU NEED NOT PIT
    YOURSELF AGAINST THESE, KNOWING THAT BECAUSE THEY
    HAVE BEEN NEAR PERFECTION, YOU TOO MUST BE.

LH Whatever it is, it feels hand-picked, not more than 20 or
    25 souls out of the whole myriads of people. And al-
    though they have died, they don't feel like they have died
    a cruel death, nor have they inflicted it, but it feels fine.
    Don't worry if you're not one of them. You don't seem
    to be and neither do I.

PB Here is my final question: If the Communists go, will
    there be others to perpetuate crimes against man?

S   YES, FOR YOU MUST REMEMBER THAT AT ALL STAGES OF LIFE
    THERE ARE SOULS THAT HAVE NOT MADE THEIR TOTAL

EVOLVEMENT. AS LONG AS THESE ARE YET UPON THE EARTH PLANE, OR THOSE WHO NEED TO INCARNATE, THESE PROBLEMS WILL CONTINUE TO ARISE. THIS IS NOT TOTAL FOR ALL TIME, HOWEVER, FOR THIS IS BEING WEEDED AWAY.

PB That should be enough for today. Thank you very much.

LH Do you have a lot more questions?

PB Yes, long lists, but we'll go through them as you have the time.

LH The only problem is that there are two other men doing research through my Source and that takes my time, but it is very different material than what interests you. One is exploring the causes of crib deaths and the other future earthquakes.

(With that we made an appointment for the following week and thanked her again.)

The second appointment had to be postponed for three weeks because Lenora's daughter went into the hospital for surgery, and with construction of new houses cut back sharply, her husband was out of work. In spite of this, she fitted some people in. She would never charge for her services, but some people were generous and these funds helped in their troubled times.

When we did come back together, she seemed like an old friend, and we looked forward to further illumination on Peter's brilliant list of questions.

As before, her house was immaculate, and we caught a glimpse of a little figure in a bathrobe disappearing through the kitchen door, her head swathed in bandages.

"How is your daughter getting along?" Peter asked.

"We're so glad to have her home from the hospital. It's been very difficult, but somehow we are given the strength we need." She gave us a tired smile which was so appealing I wanted to put my arms around her.

"Do you feel up to this session?"

"Oh, yes. This is the part of my life that's most interesting. If only I had more TIME for it."

With that Peter checked his tape recorder and she picked up her pen in readiness.

He was just about to ask his first question when the telephone rang.

"Oh, I'm so sorry," she said as she headed for the kitchen. In a few minutes she was back. "I'm going to have to do something about that. Your time shouldn't be taken by strangers making appointments."

Once again she sat down and composed herself with her eyes closed. When she opened them, with her pen in hand, already making the circles, Peter started:

PB   We are concerned about our daughter.

(Lenora, who didn't even know we had a daughter, explained:)

LH   If you want to ask some questions about her, just give me an initial and we'll see what comes.

PB   What do you see in A's problems?

LH   I keep feeling like she's trying something and doesn't succeed. She can't get over the hump. She's having a traumatic time with her own inner consciousness and a good deal of debate as to whether she's in her right place—or on her right path—on this earth at this time. She needs to settle back into her situation and know that she has a good lesson here that can be coped with. She has all of the material needs that are helpful in working this out. Her leaping around seems to be running away rather than accepting or settling in.

(It was interesting to see how differently this personal material came through than that on a more academic level. In this case Lenora seemed to get feelings and pictures, but was surely identifying the case properly. There could be no doubt that the entity concerned was our restless daughter. The last we had heard, unknown to Lenora, was that she was leaving her third husband.)

PB Will she find guidance that will send her back to the situation she needs to face?

LH The guidance feels like it's already there, but she can't bring it up to look at it. She can't see the actual thing that she needs to work with . . .

PB Has she faced this same problem in other lives?

LH It feels like the two preceding this. It's a repeat performance. She needs to stay with this and solve it in this life. Encourage her. Help her. Guide her. Teach her those things you know and she will come to her own conclusion. She has good intellectual ability.

PB How can I teach someone who is not listening?

LH You keep dropping the words and she isn't listening, but it's going down into the depths of her and it seems to come back up and she thinks, 'oh, that's my own idea.' But if you suggested it, she'd push away.

PB Does she need to stay in the same geographical location with the same people to work it out?

LH That island is very important, and seems to go back to a past life as though that territory played an important part then. As to her husband, if she doesn't work it out with him, there will be someone else, but it seems to be more emotionally uncomfortable with someone else.

PB   Is there anything specific her mother can do for her?

LH   Her mother—this is her mother, isn't it?—seems to listen with a sympathetic ear and this is something she has need for. I feel the coming together of understanding and compassion. This daughter of yours does not feel quite ready to learn this lesson. You seem to become like a school teacher or a disciplinarian, and she's not ready for that now. It's a lack of desire to control herself.

I don't feel your shoulder there for her to cry on. I'm not saying that you wouldn't be good for her. It's just that you wouldn't accomplish what her mother would, and this is what makes her comfortable. She has all the equipment to be a stable person, but she is not desiring at this time to be one who can be depended upon or relied on. She has a desire to run away from things. Be patient with her. She has a long road ahead. She will continue to make progress. Be patient.

PB   Thank you. What lessons do I have to learn in this life?

LH   Trust seems to be one—trust of others' opinions and abilities, as well as your own.

(I had to laugh within at this because he was such a strong and determined businessman who felt nothing would be done properly unless he himself had done it.)
Then she continued:

LH   You have a great deal of know-how within you, and it is difficult to entrust important details to other people. You seem to have already developed patience, but it is very martial. As though as long as I watch it, I can be patient.

That's all. I'm sure you have others, but I can't seem to find them.

(I was anxious to learn about my own.)

JB What lessons do *I* have in this life?

LH Asserting yourself. You need to be more positive with those steps that you take so you can trust your own judgment. You have a desire to do this and a knowing within you when you are right. It is only necessary that you stand up more firmly for this.

(Because the style of speaking was unlike that of the academic information before, it was difficult to determine if any of this should be put in all caps, but I had the feeling that it came authoritatively from a source other than Lenora. She herself did not know anything about us personally and here she was able to see within us, describing one of the weakest links in my character. This time I laughed at myself. Then Lenora went on:)

And if there's anything you love, it feels like it's truth. Truth from anyone.
I'm not trying to give you more lessons than your husband, but you need to learn stick-to-it-ive-ness.

JB That's certainly true. Asserting myself has always been difficult. May I ask another question?
Since my family are very short-lived, will I die before I am 60?

LH I don't feel it. You have no need for an early death. In this life there is a great deal yet to be done. You are one who is able to balance things out, and although you are somewhat observing things, this is what you are here for.

(Once again I was amazed, because I am a Libra, the sign of the scales, and my life as a writer depends very much on observation. There was even a satisfying reassurance that this was my role.)

PB I'd like to get back to your Source with questions about UFO's. Could he tell us their source, purpose, intent and so on.

S   THESE ARE THE TRAVELLING VEHICLES OF OTHER WORLDS. THEY ARE NOT TO BE FEARED GREATLY, BUT THERE ARE THOSE AREAS THAT ARE GREATLY MISUNDERSTOOD BY THE HUMANS. THERE ARE A FEW WITHIN THESE SPACE VEHICLES WHOSE INTENT AND PURPOSES ARE NOT THE HIGHEST, AND YET THEY WILL NOT CAUSE A DEFORMITY TO THE EARTH. THEY TRAVEL IN MUCH THE MANNER THAT MAN ON THIS EARTH HAS BEEN ABLE TO CONCEIVE OF, AND YET HAS NOT BROUGHT TO PASS YET. HE ALREADY HAS THE INSTRUMENTS, THE POWER, THE IMAGINATION THAT HAS PLACED THESE ON DRAWING BOARDS, BUT HAS NOT YET SENT THEM INTO THE ETHERS.

    THERE IS ALSO AN AREA OF SPACE VEHICLE THAT IS NOT VISIBLE TO THE MATERIAL EYE, BUT IS MORE A THOUGHT FORM. HOWEVER, THAT ONE WHICH IS VISIBLE TO THE EYE IS ONE WHICH MANY HAVE CATALOGUED AND FEAR GREATLY. THESE ARE FROM WITHIN THE UNIVERSE IN WHICH YOU RESIDE.

LH They are saying PLUTO or PLUTONIC or something.

S   THEY ARE KEEPING AN EVER-WATCHFUL EYE UPON THE WORKINGS OF MANKIND. THEY ARE STANDING BY. THEY SHALL NOT INTERFERE AS YET, BUT ARE GATHERING MUCH INFORMATION.

LH They seem to shake their heads and wonder that more has not been destroyed.

PB Is this communication at this level a constructive purpose for us at this time?

LH It says, NOT NECESSARY.

S YOU HAVE THE KNOWING WITHIN YOU THAT THESE ARE BEINGS WHICH ARE NOT HARMFUL TO YOU NOR YOUR PURPOSES. YOU NEED NOT BE GREATLY CONCERNED, FOR YOU ARE WORKING IN ESSENCE FOR THE SAME END THAT THEY ARE.

PB Will a population thinning-out take place because of a self-inflicted catastrophe?

S MAN INFLICTS MANY THINGS UPON HIMSELF OF WHICH HE IS NOT AWARE. MANY OF THE CATASTROPHES WHICH COME ARE BECAUSE MAN IS SO VERY NEGATIVE IN HIS THINKING AND SO VERY VIOLENT AND . . . ANTI . . . IN HIS ACTIONS. THE CAUSATIONS ARE NOT ALWAYS OUTWARD OR OUTSIDE.

   MAN AS MIND IS ONE OF THE MOST IMPORTANT FACTORS IN BRINGING DISASTER OR CATASTROPHE. THESE ARE NOT ESSENTIAL OR NECESSARY IN KEEPING THE BALANCE OF NATURE. THESE ARE BECAUSE MAN HAS HELPED TO BRING THEM ABOUT.

PB It seems to me that man is, in fact, creating complexities in life that he will eventually be unable to cope with, which could cause a famine or plague that would thin out the population. Could this be right?

S AMEN!

PB What about the earth changing on its axis?

LH That seems to come and it feels like it's in the 1990's.

PB Is it greatly damaging?

S No.

LH Startling, upsetting, surprising, but it doesn't seem to destroy a lot.

PB Is there a great plan of the Brotherhoods?

S   THEY HAVE ALWAYS BEEN AT WORK TO UNFOLD THE BEAUTY
    THAT IS WITHIN MAN, TO MAKE HIM COME FORWARD TO
    WORK AND ACT IN HIS HIGHEST WAY, TO BRING ABOUT ON
    EARTH THOSE THINGS WHICH ARE ALREADY TAKING PLACE
    ON THE HIGHER PLANES. THEY HAVE ALWAYS SOUGHT TO
    MAKE MAN BECOME.

PB Do the outstanding spiritual leaders of the world really
    carry a particular message needed in the particular time,
    place and culture in which they appear?

S   YES, AND AS IS OFTEN THE CASE, THE WHOLE WORLD TRIES
    TO TAKE UP THE CRY OF ONE BATTLE. THEY FORGET THAT
    MANY OF THE THINGS WHICH ARE GIVEN TO ONE AREA ARE
    NOT NECESSARILY USEFUL OR BENEFICIAL TO ANOTHER AREA.
    HOWEVER, IF THEY WOULD TAKE THE PEARL OF GREAT PRICE
    OR THE BIT OF WISDOM AND TRUTH THAT IS WITHIN THE
    TEACHING, THEY WOULD THEN BE ABLE TO APPLY IT TO THEIR
    OWN AREA WITHOUT TRANSFERRING THE CULTURE OF THAT
    THROUGH WHICH IT HAS COME.

PB Moses is considered to have brought the law. Jesus
    brought the concept of love and, quote, "You are as you
    think." Is this evaluation correct?

S   MOSES BROUGHT THE LAW AS MAN HAD NEED OF IT AT THAT
    TIME. JESUS CAME TO FULFILL THIS LAW AND TO CONTINUE
    TO HAVE MAN OBSERVE IT. HOWEVER, IT DID NOT NEED TO
    BE TO THE LETTER OR IN THE FINITENESS. . . .

LH That's the wrong word . . . it's in the littleness . . .

S   IN THE LITTLENESS OF IT. BUT HE ALSO WANTED MAN TO
    RULE WITH HIS HEART AND WITH HIS MIND. THIS IS MOST
    NECESSARY, FOR IT IS ESSENTIAL THAT ALL THE AREAS OF
    MAN BE OPEN, ALL THE CENTERS WITHIN HIM.

PB What other concepts are to follow?

S   EACH SOUL OR ENTITY MUST FOLLOW THAT WHICH IS COR-
RECT FOR HIS OWN BEING. HE MUST FIND THAT HE NEEDS TO
LIVE WITHIN THE FRAMEWORK OF HIS SOCIETY AT THE TIME
HE IS IN THAT PARTICULAR ENVIRONMENT. IT IS ALSO NECES-
SARY THAT HE TREAT HIS FELLOW MAN IN SUCH A MANNER
THAT HE DOES NOT SUPPRESS HIS GROWTH. IT IS NECESSARY
THAT HE LOVE HIMSELF AND HIS BROTHER, LOVE HIS COUN-
TRY AND HIS WORLD, LOVE HIS GOD OR THE FORCE FROM
WITHOUT. HE NEEDS TO BECOME AT ONE WITH ALL THINGS.

LH When I say that, the human body seems to disintegrate
and it just becomes air, like all-in-all.

PB Was Jesus Christ really the force that many Christian
people attribute to him?

S   HE WAS AND IS THE SON OF GOD, BUT SO ARE ALL WHO WALK
THE EARTH. IT IS NECESSARY THAT MAN TAKE UP HIS BANNER
AND REALIZE THAT HE TOO IS A SON OF THE LIVING GOD,
THAT HE WALK WITH HIS HEAD HELD HIGH, THAT HE USE HIS
POWERS EVEN AS GOD WOULD USE HIS POWERS OF MIND
OVER MATTER. IT IS NECESSARY THAT THIS BE DONE.

PB Good. Now, some people believe that the force or
vibration left by Jesus Christ is the single most powerful
force available to man here and now. Please explain as
to the accuracy and validity of this concept.

S   MAN HAS WITHIN HIMSELF THE POTENTIAL OF BECOMING A
CHRIST CONSCIOUSNESS AND, IN THIS SENSE, HE IS THEN
RAISED TO THAT VIBRATION WHICH CHRIST HIMSELF HELD
WHILE ON THE EARTH. HIS VIBRATION IS STILL HERE ONLY AS
HIS WORDS AND THOSE WHO CARRY THEM THROUGH QUOTE
"IN HIS NAME" IS ACCOMPLISHED. THIS IS THE VIBRATION
AND THE POWER THAT HE LEFT BEHIND. HE IS WITH THE
WORLD AT ALL TIMES IN THE CONSCIOUS STATE. THIS IS ALSO
RECOGNIZED AS THE CHRIST CONSCIOUSNESS. MAN HAS THE
KEY TO UNLOCK THIS DOOR IF HE WILL BUT ACCEPT THIS.
HOWEVER, HE PREFERS TO REST BACK AND LET CHRIST,

QUOTE "ACCEPT ALL THE RESPONSIBILITY" AND LOAD OF
THOSE THINGS WHICH HE COULD HELP ACCOMPLISH AND
BRING ABOUT AN EVEN MORE RAPID RETURN OF, QUOTE,
"THE KINGDOM."

PB Is the Truth a constantly changing thing?

S No. IT IS EMBROIDERED DIFFERENTLY IN MANY MANNERS IN
MANY COUNTRIES. HOWEVER, BASIC TRUTH IS ALWAYS
THERE. LOVE, PEACE, HUMILITY, POWER, ENERGY, THESE ARE
PARTS OF TRUTH. TRUTH IS ALL THERE IS. IT IS NOT THE
MATERIAL PART OF THE WORLD NOR THE ABSTRACT WHICH
CAUSE HARM OR LESSER GOOD TO COME TO OTHER SOULS.
TRUTH IS THAT WHICH GOD IS. TRUTH IS IN ABUNDANCE.
HOWEVER, MAN IS AT VARYING DEGREES OF RECOGNIZING
TRUTH OR OF BEING ABLE TO EXPRESS IT.

PB How many at this level comprehend Truth?

S THOSE WHO ARE MASTERS AND ARE READY TO LEAVE THIS
PLANE OF GROWTH HAVE BEEN ABLE TO ACCEPT MUCH OF
TRUTH. BUT EVEN THEY DO NOT FULLY COMPREHEND ITS
MEANING. THEY ARE MASTERS OF BEING ABLE TO WORK WITH
IT ON THE EARTH'S LEVEL AND THEY ACCEPT MUCH OF WHAT
THEY DO NOT RECOGNIZE.

LH Truth does not seem to change, but man seems to keep
growing toward it. Truth seems to be this All. And even
when they leave this earth plane, they seem to still be
growing in awareness of what it is.

As Lenora's voice finished answering that question, Peter
looked up from his list. She was waiting expectantly, but he
decided this had been enough drain on her energies.

"That clarified a lot," he said with satisfaction. "Let's stop
for today and continue on Monday."

Lenora looked at her schedule for a suitable time and we
walked out to our car, feeling we'd been for a part of a day in
a different realm. It was somewhat difficult to bring ourselves
back.

Once again we had made the hour's drive from the San Francisco Bay Area to San Jose. In spite of his own busy schedule, Peter was strongly motivated to go on with his questioning. Lenora made times on three days a week for us to communicate with this unseen "Source."

Looking modest and obliging, Lenora sat across from us at the table. She was almost prayerful in her role of go-between.

PB My first question is about energy. Is energy a fixed, universal, indestructible force which may only be converted in a prefixed, orderly manner?

S ENERGY IS AS YOU HAVE SAID. HOWEVER, IT CAN BE CONVERTED AND BECOME A DESTRUCTIVE THING EVEN AS THE ATOM CAN BE CONVERTED AND USED FOR DESTRUCTION. IT WILL NOT CONVERT ITSELF. IT MUST BE DONE AT THE HANDS OF MIND.

PB Can the speed of light be exceeded?

LH It says "YES, EASILY."

PB At this level?

LH It says, "IT IS COMING."

PB Are there many forms of matter unknown to us?

S YES. AND YET THEY ARE NOT NEW. THEY HAVE ALWAYS BEEN. THEY WILL ALWAYS BE.

PB Is there negative energy and negative matter or anti-matter and anti-energy?

LH It says "NO." Again this word, Mind, with a capital M, comes as though it converts energy and matter to this, but that doesn't seem to be a primary thing or already there.

PB To change the subject now. By society's standards, some people seem to leave reality. That is, they are con-

sidered to be unable to face "reality." Are these people
genuinely disassociated or displaced, or do they, in fact,
turn to Universal Mind at a different level?

S   THIS IS DIFFICULT TO ANSWER AS A VERY GENERAL QUES-
     TION, BECAUSE THERE ARE THOSE WHO DO REFUSE TO FACE
     REALITY AND WHO DO CARE TO DROP OUT OR DROP BACK,
     FINDING THAT THIS REALM OF, AS THE WORLD CALLS IT,
     "UNREALITY," IS MORE FAMILIAR TO THEM BECAUSE IT RE-
     LATES VERY MUCH TO THAT IN-BETWEEN PERIOD THAT THEY
     HAD EXPERIENCED BEFORE COMING TO THE EARTH, AND FIND
     THIS IS A COMFORTABLE SITUATION FOR THEM. HOWEVER,
     THOSE WHO HAVE REACHED THE HIGHER STAGES OF EVOLVE-
     MENT AND ARE ABLE TO TUNE TO HIGHER MUSIC, ARE ALSO
     CONSIDERED OUT OF IT BY THE WORLD. THESE ARE THOSE
     WHO CAN TUNE TO OTHER AREAS AND DO KNOW THE USE OF
     THE HIGHER SPIRITUAL GIFTS AND ABILITIES.

PB   Is it necessary to stay tuned in at this level to complete
     this chapter of growth?

S   YES. IT IS NECESSARY FOR YOU TO KEEP YOUR FEET CON-
     STANTLY WALKING THE EARTH PLANE, FOR ONLY BY DOING
     THIS ARE YOU ABLE TO RELATE TO OTHER PEOPLE SO THAT YOU
     CAN HELP THEM ALONG THE PATH. IT IS NOT NECESSARY FOR
     YOU TO CARRY THE WEIGHT FOR THEM, BUT IT IS NECESSARY
     FOR YOU TO BE THE GO-BETWEEN, AND BY KEEPING YOUR FEET
     IN WHAT APPEARS TO BE REALITY, YOU SET THE EXAMPLE
     THAT THEY MAY SEE BOTH YOU AND THE BEYOND.

PB   Does man's group conscience affect the physical condi-
     tion and circumstances of the earth?

S   YES, VERY MUCH SO. AS THOSE UPON THE EARTH PLANE
     RAISE OR LOWER THEIR OWN CONSCIOUSNESS, SO THE EARTH
     ITSELF IS AFFECTED. THERE IS THE NEGATIVE AND THE
     POSITIVE PULL, AND THESE ARE THE THINGS WHICH BRING
     ABOUT EITHER EARTHQUAKES OR TIDAL WAVES OR THE GROW-

ING OF GREEN THINGS. IT IS VERY NECESSARY THAT MAN BE AWARE OF HIS CONSCIOUSNESS AND OF THOSE AROUND HIM.

PB   Does man's group conscience seem to decline as mechanization and civilization advance and accelerate?

S   NOT NECESSARILY, DEPENDING UPON HOW MAN, AS SUCH, USES HIS FREE TIME. THOSE WHO ARE SEEKING INTO THE HIGHER REALMS ARE THOSE WHO ARE ABLE TO RAISE THE CONSCIOUSNESS. THOSE WHO ARE USING MECHANIZATION AS A RELEASE FROM THOUGHT ARE NOT NECESSARILY HELPING THE GENERAL AREA.

PB   Define consciousness and conscience.

(The answer came in a flash.)

S   CONSCIENCE, CONSCIOUSNESS, IS THE FULL AWARENESS. THERE ARE TWO LEVELS OF CONSCIOUSNESS. ONE IS CONSIDERED THAT OF WHICH MAN IS AWARE. THE OTHER IS A STATE THAT HIS SOUL RESIDES IN. AS HE PROGRESSES IN CONSCIOUSNESS, HIS SOUL TRAVELS UP THESE STEPS.

(Once again Lenora explained what she was getting.)

LH   And the words "CONSCIOUSNESS AS MAN IS AWARE". . . this seems to be mentally aware . . . has to do with conscience, because I seem to bounce out with consciousness and then there is a screen so I can't see through it.

PB   Let me ask this in a different way. Describe the various levels of consciousness, such as conscious, subconscious, superconscious, unconscious and any others.

S   THE CONSCIOUS MIND IS THAT WITH WHICH YOU WORK KNOWINGLY AND WILLINGLY. THIS IS THE PART OF YOUR MIND THAT YOU USE CONSTANTLY EACH DAY. THE SUBCONSCIOUS PART OF YOUR MIND IS THAT WHICH HAS BEEN CONDITIONED FROM PAST REFLEXES, PAST TIMES. THESE CAN BE PAST AS FAR AS THE CURRENT LIFE OR EVEN INFLUENCED BY

RECENT PAST LIVES. THIS IS A PART THAT CAN BE RECONDI-
TIONED TO HELP YOU THINK MORE POSITIVELY ON THE CON-
SCIOUS LEVEL. IT IS LARGELY RESPONSIBLE FOR MANY OF
YOUR CONSCIOUS RESPONSES. IT IS A VEHICLE THROUGH
WHICH YOU CAN RECEIVE OUTSIDE INFORMATION. IT IS ALSO
NOT SELECTIVE IN ITS RECEIVING, FOR MUCH THAT COMES TO
IT CAN BE CONVERTED INTO ENERGY OR LACK OF ENERGY,
MASS OR LACK OF MASS, WITHIN THAT PARTICULAR SUBCON-
SCIOUS MIND.

(Lenora looked puzzled.)

LH I thought subconscious and unconscious were the same,
but this says:

S   THE UNCONSCIOUS MIND IS THAT PART OF YOU WHICH IS AT
WORK DILIGENTLY THROUGH THE DREAM STATE AND
THROUGH YOUR DEEPENING MEDITATIVE STATES. IT IS THE
PART WHICH RULES THE REFLEXES, THE PART WHICH IS TRUE
TO YOURSELF REGARDLESS OF . . .

(Now she had to explain again.)

LH And this seems to be where the subconscious separates
from it. The unconscious mind feels true to you. The
subconscious seems to waver interchangeably.

S   THE SUPERCONSCIOUS IS THAT PART OF MAN WHICH RELATES
TO THE GOD OR THE UNIVERSAL PART WITHOUT. IT IS THE
HIGH SELF, THAT WHICH WOULD DO NOTHING TO HARM
THAT PARTICULAR ENTITY. IT IS THE PART THAT IS IN CON-
TACT WITH THE SOUL AND THE OVERSPIRIT. IT IS THE PART
THROUGH WHICH MAN CAN RECEIVE HIGHEST VIBRATIONS
AND CAN CONVERT THESE INTO ENERGY FOR HIS OWN
PHYSICAL WELL BEING, FOR HIS OWN HEALING.

PB Thank you. Now, it seems as though each time they get
civilization advanced and mechanized, it sort of goes
over the top, and then everything falls apart. Is that a
historical thing?

LH When you were talking about it just now, it felt like we reached this peak, and this seems to be where mechanization takes over, and some of the people seem to be going on up, and some feel like they drop back down.

PB I'm wondering about mankind as a whole.

LH All right. Let's see. Mankind as a whole.

S THIS IS A PATTERN, AS SUCH, AND YET THERE IS ALSO A BREAKING TIME. THIS CAN BE THE TIME WHEN THOSE WHO LIFT THEIR CONSCIOUSNESS CAN FAR OUTWEIGH THOSE WHO REFUSE TO SEEK OR TO LOOK. THIS IS AGAIN A PERIOD IN HISTORY WHEN FREE WILL WILL BE AN IMPORTANT PART OF ALL MANKIND AND THEIR AWARENESS.

PB We are at a crossroad now?

S RIGHT.

(Peter, dark and intense, was looking through his notes to see what he wanted next. His questions were all unknown to me, and so, like Lenora, I was as fascinated by his range as I was by the profundity of the answers. Now he changed to another theme.)

PB Why is it that, other than current Japan, all material progress seems to have been caused by northern Europeans?

S THERE HAS BEEN A HIGHER DEVELOPMENT OF MIND POWER WITH THOSE FROM THE EUROPEAN AREA, WHILE THOSE IN JAPAN ARE USING A MEDITATIVE FORM. THUS IT IS THAT THE ACTION OR THE MIND POWER ONES HAVE COME FORTH TO HELP A GREAT DEAL. JAPAN HAS HELPED THEMSELVES, AND MANKIND ALSO, BUT AT A SLOWER PACE.

LH They seem to meditate and think on it, and then work on things that have come through. Does that make sense?

PB   Well, they have an industrialized society and they are surpassing us or catching up with us at a very rapid rate.

LH   Yes, but it feels like their background of meditation or quiet or serenity has been the thing that lets the wheels work. First, when you mentioned Europe, I feel honed or steel-sharp, or high-keyed, as though these are the things of mind power. I don't feel heart or meditation or anything tied with those.

PB   I wonder if this is really progress.

S   ONLY IN THAT IT CAN RELEASE OR FREE PEOPLE TO DO THOSE THINGS WHICH ARE NECESSARY. IF THIS MIND POWER HAS BEEN ABLE TO RELEASE THEM TO USE THEIR OWN MIND POWER TO GREATER ADVANTAGE OR IN A BENEFICIAL MANNER, THEN THIS IS PROGRESS. HOWEVER, IF IT IS USED STRICTLY TO FIND FREE TIME OR TO UTILIZE IN SUCH A WAY AS WILL HURT YOUR FELLOW MAN, THEN THIS IS NOT PROGRESS.

PB   Does human earth life have to be longer in years to progress?

LH   It says you already know the answer to this.

S   YOU HAVE WITNESSED MANY WHO ARE ELDERLY AND YET ARE NOT ABLE TO PROGRESS. YOU HAVE WITNESSED THOSE WHO ARE YOUNG AND ABLE TO SEE THE DEPTH FAR BEYOND THOSE OF EVEN YOUR OWN AGE. KNOW THAT EARTH YEARS ARE NOT IMPORTANT, BUT TIMES UPON THE EARTH CAN BE EXTREMELY IMPORTANT BECAUSE THEY WILL BRING ABOUT THE PERIODS OF GROWTH TO EACH INDIVIDUAL SOUL.

PB   Now, I'd like to ask some questions about healing. Is man really self-healing?

S   HE CAN BE. ONLY AS HE IS A PART OF THE TOTAL OR THE WHOLE, AS HE IS A PART OF GOD . . .

     (Lenora interrupted at this point.)

LH   That's my own interpretation: God.

S   . . . As he is a part of all the forces thus he is able to bring that force in himself, for perfection is the true being of all things.

PB Is God actually a Universal Intelligence at a certain level —possibly a level attuned to each seeking entity?

S   God, referred to by most people, is a very low entity in comparison to that which he is. God, as such, is the prevailing force or power, the ultimate energy or vibration of the universe as man now knows it. This is all within his keeping. There is not a separate God or entity for each planet or earth.

PB What are vibrations?

LH I'm not seeing a particular color. I'm seeing a color and a musical note, and I get the word, harmony.

S   These are the manifestations of the vibratory rates of energy. These are the energy impulses which come either as a form of sight or sound. You would find that these could harmonize with each other, that the sight could always be interpreted into a sound and vice versa. They are also the feelings that reach people.

LH Ah, and I feel heat or color as much as hearing it.

PB I'm not thinking of vibrations as man knows them, but vibrations in the universal sense.

S   Energy!

PB Vibrations are energy? Is energy life?

LH Vibrations seem to be energy, but energy is not . . . let's see . . . life is not a total word for energy. Life feels partial . . . like three-quarters of energy, but there seems to be something else in there.
(Lenora was looking out the window.)
I don't seem to be getting this. It's very far away.

(And with that she picked up her pen and started making the tunnels of circles. Still nothing came. When Peter saw she was having trouble with it, he decided to move on to another question.)

PB   That's all right. We'll try something else.
      What exactly is odor?

S   IT IS A PARTIAL FORMATION OF ENERGY THAT HAS BEEN DISPERSED OR SENT OFF BY ONE PARTICULAR ITEM SUCH AS A VEGETABLE WHEN COOKING OR A PERSON WHEN RUNNING OR A ROSE WHEN BLOOMING. IT IS AN ESSENCE . . . AN ENERGY MASS OR PARTICLES OF ENERGY. AND THROUGH THIS IT CAN BE DETECTED OR DENOTE PRESENCE.

LH   That's all I get.

PB   Is odor vibration?

LH   No, I get energy because it feels more like moving.

S   IT IS ENERGY WHICH IS A FORM OF VIBRATION. ALL THINGS THAT ARE TERMED ENERGY CAN ALSO BE TERMED VIBRATION. HOWEVER, THESE TWO TERMS ARE NOT REALLY INTERCHANGEABLE.

PB   Do certain odors increase an entity's accuity on the spirit level?

S   THESE CERTAIN ODORS ARE ABLE TO SPEAK TO FINER ELEMENTS WITHIN MAN OR CALL FORTH FORGOTTEN MEMORIES, WHICH IS EXTREMELY IMPORTANT, FOR MANY TIMES THIS CAN CALL FORTH PERHAPS A RELIGIOUS EXPERIENCE OR ONE OF UPLIFTING TIME IN DISTANT PAST.

LH   And this doesn't feel like this life, but past lives that would be most beneficial.

S   MANY ODORS ARE CONDUCIVE TO SPIRIT MANIFESTATIONS OR MELTING WITH, INTERSPERSING, OF A HIGHER ODOR.

PB   What entities are identified by odor?

S ALL ENTITIES ARE IDENTIFIED BY THIS, FOR IT IS A MATTER OF VIBRATION OR ENERGY THAT COMES FORTH FROM ANY SOURCE. HOWEVER, NOT ALL ENTITIES OR PEOPLE ARE ABLE TO DISCERN THIS OR TO SMELL IT. SOME ARE ABLE TO SMELL FLOWERS VERY WELL. OTHERS DO NOT NOTICE THE ODOR. SOME ARE ABLE TO SMELL SPIRIT OR SPIRIT MANIFESTATIONS, WHILE OTHERS ARE NOT AWARE OF THIS AT ALL. ALL COLOR, SIGHT AND SMELL IS VIBRATION AND ENERGY COMING FORTH, AND THUS IT IS APPARENT TO SOMEONE AT SOME LEVEL.

PB Thank you. May we go on to the subject of spiritual healing? I would like to know if this is through a force within the entity being healed or from outside?

S THIS AGAIN IS NOT ONE PAT ANSWER, FOR THERE ARE MANY AREAS IN WHICH IT IS NECESSARY THAT AN OUTSIDE FORCE COME. ALMOST AS THOUGH IT IS AN ELECTRICAL CHARGE FROM ANOTHER BEING. HOWEVER, THIS USUALLY IS A CASE OF AN OUTSIDE FORCE TAPPING OR PLUGGING INTO THAT WHICH IS WITHIN THE BEING.

THOSE WHO ARE UNABLE TO MANIFEST THEIR OWN HEALING FROM WITHIN, WHOSE ENERGY CHARGE IS SO LOW THAT IT IS NOT SUFFICIENT TO CAUSE A HEALING, MUST BE REINFORCED BY AN OUTSIDE REACHING IN.

PB Can an entity be helped if he is not seeking help for himself?

S THERE IS A MEASURE OF HELP WHICH COMES IN THE AURA AROUND HIM. HOWEVER, THIS IS NOT OF DIRECT BENEFIT, FOR HE MUST BE SEEKING BEFORE HIS MIND IS TRULY OPEN, AND AT THAT POINT HE CAN THEN GATHER TO HIMSELF THE INFORMATION THAT WILL LAST THROUGH THE AGES. THE HELP IS MEASURED.

PB Can an entity control accidents, violence, discomfort, danger, etc. through his own thinking?

S   TO SOME DEGREE. HOWEVER, WHEN ONE IS CLOSELY INTE-
     GRATED WITH OTHERS AROUND HIM, THE THINKING OF
     OTHERS WILL ALSO HELP TO INFLUENCE THE THINGS WHICH
     ARE ACTIVATED WITHIN THE ENTITY'S LIFE.

PB   Is there a way that these problems can be effectively met
     if they appear? Or should they be avoided in the first
     place?

S   NO, THEY SHOULD NOT BE AVOIDED, FOR IT IS NECESSARY TO
     MEET ANYTHING HEAD-ON SO THAT YOU MAY TEST YOUR
     OWN STRENGTH, SO THAT YOU MAY ALSO HELP OTHERS WHO
     ARE ALSO INVOLVED WITHIN THE PARTICULAR NEED AT THE
     TIME.

LH   And I get a feeling of seeing a problem and then a piece
     of macaroni. Like it goes in your eyes and out the top of
     your head. See the problem. Don't dwell on it. Don't
     judge it. But lift it immediately into God's presence.

PB   Is man truly complete with all his needs met from his in-
     ception?

S   THE ANSWERS ARE ABOUT HIM. IT IS HIS DUTY AND
     RIGHTFUL POSSESSION TO BE ABLE TO CHANNEL THESE AN-
     SWERS TO HIS OWN NEED. THE ANSWER IS ALWAYS THERE.
     THE SOLUTION IS THERE FOR THE PROBLEM.

PB   Can healing prayers generate greater force with a group
     effort?

S   YES. THERE IS THE FORMING TOGETHER OF A MORE POWER-
     FUL KNOT OF COMMUNICATIONS, A LINE THAT IS MORE DI-
     RECT. THERE IS THE FULLNESS OF ACCEPTANCE WHERE ONE
     PERSON WHO PRAYS ALONE MANY TIMES DOES NOT HAVE THE
     STRENGTH OR THE POWER TO REACH OUT BY HIMSELF. MUCH
     OF WHAT MAN ALONE PRAYS FOR IS COUNTERACTED BY HIS
     OWN LACK OF BELIEF OR ACCEPTANCE. MANY IN A GROUP
     ADD TO THE ABUNDANCE AND LOVE THAT CAN FLOW THROUGH
     TO THAT GROUP AND TO OTHERS THROUGH THEM.

LH There is a far greater opening . . . more facets. Again this glittering ball that I see so many times. More parts who see it differently.

PB How can one best raise one's vibration level to accomplish healing?

S DESIRE TO SEE ALL THAT IS GOOD IN ALL THINGS, ALL PEOPLE, ALL PLACES, ALL SITUATIONS, SEEKING TO SEE THE HEALING OF THE NATIONS OF THE WORLD, OF ALL THAT IS, WILL BE A PART OF THE GENERAL THINKING THAT IS NECESSARY BEFORE ONE CAN SEE CRAWLING SORES OR OPEN WOUNDS AS WHOLE. IT IS NECESSARY TO OVERLOOK OR TO SEE THE TOTAL RATHER THAN TO CONCENTRATE ON THE SMALL THINGS.

LH I'm seeing a newspaper picture instead of concentrating on the little dots that go to make up the picture. I see the image that it's trying to project. So it's saying that as you're trying to raise your own vibrations, when you see a person, don't even think, 'Well, I don't like the color of his necktie, or I don't like the way she wears those shoes', or see any of the flaw. It's like look into the eyes or look into the soul. And even if you don't see what you want to see or see what you like, try to picture that. If nothing else, put a Christ face . . . and I use this because I'm a Christian . . . put a Christ face there and then I can feel myself using a car jack to jack myself up.

PB You said "a Christ face" and I'm wondering what you are visualizing.

S CHRIST IS. CHRIST IS THAT SOURCE OR LIGHT OR PART OF GOD WHICH YOU WOULD ENVISION TO BE OF A BEAUTIFUL NATURE, BE IT BLACK, WHITE, YELLOW OR RED. BE AWARE IT IS THE LOVE WHICH SHINES THROUGH THE EYES, THE WHOLENESS, THE PURITY, AND NOT THE OUTWARD APPEARANCE. THIS IS WHERE YOU LEARN TO LOOK BEYOND THE FACE, AND I KNOW THAT YOU KNOW THAT.

PB Are prayers for a nation, a city, a society etc. helpful?

S   NECESSARY!

PB To more than just the conscience of the individual doing the praying?

S   YES. THESE GENERATE A VERY REAL AND . . .

LH It says "SEEABLE". . .
(She was often to puzzle a word that seemed unusual to her.)

S   . . . VERY REAL AND SEEABLE POWER OR ENERGY. IT IS BE-
CAUSE OF MANY OF THESE PRAYERS THAT CONDITIONS ON
EARTH HAVE BEEN CHANGED IN THE PAST, AND WILL BE CON-
TINUING TO CHANGE IN THE FUTURE. THIS IS A MUST.

PB How does prayer cause the desired changes to occur?

S   IT GENERATES AN ELECTRICAL FORCE OR IMPULSE, AN
ENERGY, THAT IS ABLE TO LIFT THE OTHER VIBRATIONS TO
SOME DEGREE, AND ENOUGH OF THESE FOCAL POINTS CAN
LIFT THE VIBRATION OF THE SAID GOVERNMENTS, COUNTRY,
STATE, GROUP. . . .

LH And it feels like the United Nations.

S   . . . TO THE EXTENT THAT THEY ARE THEN WORKING ON A
HIGHER PLANE.

PB Is the speedup in earth life conditions and world affairs meaningful?

S   IT IS IN THE CONSCIOUSNESS OF MAN THAT THIS HAS BEEN
SEEDED, FOR MAN IS BECOMING FAR MORE AWARE OF HIS
MENTAL ABILITIES AND POWERS, AND THIS IS THE REASON
THAT MUCH HAS BEEN DISCOVERED, INVENTED, RELEASED IN
THE PAST FEW YEARS. YES, IT IS MEANINGFUL. HOWEVER, IT
DOES NOT MEAN, AS MANY INTERPRET IT TO, THAT TIME IS
RUNNING OUT. IT ONLY MEANS THAT ACTION MUST TAKE
PLACE, FOR THINGS ARE MOVING AT A MORE RAPID PACE. IT

IS NECESSARY THAT MAN CONQUER HIS PHYSICAL STRENGTH TO THE POINT THAT HE CAN RULE HIS SPIRITUAL STRENGTH.

PB That seems a strong ending. Let's call it a day and continue on Friday. I have another list I am putting together for then.

LH I'll bet you DO.
(And she was laughing as she said it.)

"How good it is to see you!" Lenora welcomed. "We have happy news here. Our daughter can go back to school." We breathed a sigh of relief after they'd gone through so much. And with that brief exchange, Peter got out his notes and started his questions.

PB Some say the United States is or will be the spiritual center of the world. Is this so?

S IT HAS THE POTENTIAL, FOR THE NEED IS VERY STRONG. AND THIS IS A LAND OF GREAT SUPPLY. HOWEVER, IT IS STILL THE WILL OF THE PEOPLE. THE FORCES THAT ARE NECESSARY TO MAKE THIS THE SPIRITUAL CENTER ARE BEING DRAWN HERE EVEN AT THIS TIME. IT IS NECESSARY THAT THESE THINGS BE BROUGHT TO LIGHT. THE OFFER MADE, THE CHANCE IS GIVEN.

PB Are there various spiritual centers for various levels or planes?

LH All right. I keep getting "India, India, India"—even as you asked, "will the U.S. be the place?" And yet, when you say "centers," they don't seem to stop there. It's like they are stair steps . . . Wait a minute now . . . On the unconscious level they don't seem to be individual. They seem to be all sharing. I can't make it any clearer.

PB Well, they probably are circles within circles. Does that make sense?

S   YES.

PB And this would be true of the universe as well as the world, I presume?

S   YES. ALL THINGS WHICH ARE MANIFEST ON A VERY SMALL SCALE OR IN MINUTE ORDER ARE ALSO TRUE OF THE LARGER OR MACROCOSM.

PB Describe and define in detail the microcosm and macrocosm in the world's manifestation as we know it.

S   THE MICROCOSM, AS YOU ARE WELL AWARE, IS THE MOST MINUTE OF ALL THINGS. IT IS THE SMALLEST ATOM, THE NEUTRONS, THE PROTONS, THOSE FORCES OF ALL THINGS WHICH BECOME AS ENERGY. THESE ARE NOT VISIBLE TO THE NAKED EYE, AND YET THEY ARE AS REAL, AS COMPLETE, AS WHOLE, AS IS THE HUMAN BODY. EACH OF THESE IS IN DIRECT RELATION OR EFFECTIVENESS TO THE TOTAL OF THAT OF WHICH IT IS A PART, AS IS TRUE IN THE MACROCOSM, WHICH WOULD BE THE TOTAL OF A UNIVERSE.

LH It doesn't seem to go on into infinity, but a universe is the limit of the macrocosm.

S   AND EVEN AS THIS IS SO, YOU WILL FIND THAT THE UNIVERSES BECOME AS THE MICROCOSM TO A GREATER THING WHICH WOULD BE RECOGNIZABLE ONLY IN A FUTURE TIME. AND THEN THE UNIVERSES APPEAR AS LITTLE ATOMS. IN EACH OF THESE THINGS THERE MUST BE THE POSITIVE AND THE NEGATIVE, THE YES AND THE NO, THE GOOD AND THE BAD, AS MAN MIGHT CALL IT. THE DRAWING AND REPELLING, THE FORCE AND ANTI-FORCE. FOR ONLY THROUGH THESE CAN A TOTAL OR BALANCE BE ACCOMPLISHED. THE BALANCE IS NECESSARY THAT ALL THINGS REMAIN IN THEIR PLACE, FOR WITHOUT THIS PERFECT BALANCE THERE WOULD BE A FLYING INTO OBLIVION FOR ALL THAT HAS BEEN CREATED.

LH Was that in detail?

PB Yes. Fine. Are there beings or entities committed to preventing man and other life forms from destroying the world or the universe in its manifested forms?

S THERE ARE THOSE WHO ARE STANDING BY. THEY DO NOT CAUSE NOR COMMIT THEMSELVES TO INTERFERE. HOWEVER, SHOULD A GREAT EMERGENCY OR CATACLYSM APPROACH, THEY WOULD BE THERE TO HOLD IT BACK, DEPENDING UPON THE WILL OF MAN.

LH And this seems to be not the single will of man but the total or group will.

S THUS THE NECESSITY OF RAISING VIBRATIONS IN ANY AREA WHERE IT IS POSSIBLE. WHENEVER A POSITIVE THOUGHT IS POSSIBLE IN PLACE OF A NEGATIVE, THIS MUST BE REPLACED, FOR EACH OF THESE COMES TOGETHER TO MAKE THE WHOLE FOR A GENERAL RAISING. EVEN THOUGH IT BE SLOW, IT IS NECESSARY.

PB But the positive thought has to be a correction of the negative, not just a joyful burying of the head as it were?

S TRUE. TRUE. ONE HAS TO SEE THIS AND WILLFULLY SHIFT IT.

(Lenora had picked up her pen and was making circles as the telephone rang. "You'll be pleased to know that I now have a telephone answering service and they take my calls for me when I have people here. It's wonderful to be almost undisturbed." Peter was particularly pleased with her solution, as I knew her husband must be too.) '

PB This has been good material we've gone through, but now I'd like to change the subject a bit. Is the sex act, as we know it, a very powerful way of creating and releasing energy in a human being?

S   IT IS A VERY NECESSARY PART OF LIFE, AND IT IS ONE OF THE
    HIGHEST POINTS OF ENERGY AND REALIZATION KNOWN TO
    MAN. IT IS THAT COMPLETE ACT OF LOVE THAT IS NECESSARY.
    THE SEX ACT, IN ITSELF, IS NOT AN ACCOMPLISHMENT IF IT
    IS DONE WITHOUT THE LOVE THAT IS NECESSARY TO CONSUM-
    MATE IT AS A LIFTING OF CONSCIOUSNESS.

PB How can this energy best be directed?

S   IT SHOULD NOT BE CONSCIOUSLY DIRECTED. IT SHOULD BE AS
    SOMETHING THAT RE-ENERGIZES OR RE-VITALIZES THOSE
    SOULS WHICH ARE INVOLVED WITHIN THE FRAMEWORK OF IT
    AT THE TIME. DO NOT TRY TO CONSCIOUSLY DIRECT IT OR
    SEND IT ANYWHERE.

PB Now, I'd like to ask about cycles. Apparently we all
    have them, and I ask you to describe cycles and their
    effects.

LH Do you mean cycles of lives or cycles within a life?

PB Well, an individual has a cycle, and the world has a cy-
    cle. I'd like a description and their interrelationships.

LH Would you like me to describe the word "the"?
    (At this point we all stopped to laugh.)

S   THESE ARE NECESSARY ERAS OF TIME. THEY ARE NOT . . .

LH I'm getting a wheel that's off-center, which tells me they
    aren't even or balanced.

S   THEY ARE DIFFERENT WITH THE VARIOUS SOULS DEPENDING
    ON THE POSITIVE OR NEGATIVE ASPECTS OF THAT PARTICULAR
    SOUL.

LH In other words, one who has a very negative attitude to-
    ward life will find that he is most often on the bottom of
    the wheel as it's going down through the mud. Then
    when it comes up, it seems to flop over quickly so there
    is a very small positive side. Excuse the pictures.

S THIS PERSON WILL HAVE LONG CYCLES OF THE NEGATIVITY. IT IS POSSIBLE, HOWEVER, FOR THIS ONE TO TAKE TRAINING AND COUNSELLING AND BE ABLE TO ELEVATE HIS THINKING SO THAT THESE SAME CYCLES CAN THEN BE BALANCED IN THE SAME WAY, ONLY ON THE POSITIVE SIDE. YOU WILL FIND THAT CYCLES WITHIN A PERSON'S LIFE USUALLY RANGE WITHIN SEVEN YEAR PERIODS. BECAUSE OF THIS, THEY ARE MORE APT TO DO CERTAIN THINGS WITHIN THESE CERTAIN PERIODS. HOWEVER, ONE MAY HAVE A YEAR OR TWO ON EITHER SIDE OF THE SEVEN-YEAR PERIOD IN WHICH THEY LAP OVER OR LAG BEHIND. THIS IS A VERY INDIVIDUAL MATTER.

YOU WILL RECOGNIZE THAT THE FIRST SEVEN YEARS OF A CHILD'S LIFE ARE THE FASTEST GROWING YEARS. THESE ARE THE TIMES IN WHICH THE BODY MAKES THE GREATEST CHANGES IN STATURE.

THE SECOND SEVEN YEARS ARE THOSE IN WHICH A PERSON BEGINS TO REACH OUT INTO THE WORLD IN A MORE EFFECTIVE WAY, LEARNING WHETHER HE IS A SOUL ON HIS OWN OR CAN RELATE TO THE OUTSIDE WORLD. THESE WOULD BE THE AREAS IN WHICH YOU FIND THAT CHILDREN CHANGE INTO YOUNG ADULTS.

FROM THAT PERIOD THEY CHANGE AND REACH INTO GREATER WORLD EFFECTS FROM THE 14th TO THE 21st YEAR. AND AT THIS POINT, THE STATE WILL ALLOW THEM TO VOTE OR BECOME PART OF THE GOVERNMENT. THEY WILL BE ABLE TO TAKE THEIR OWN FREEDOM FROM THEIR FAMILY AND TAKE THEIR RESPONSIBILITIES FOR THEMSELVES UPON THEIR OWN HEADS.

THE NEXT PERIOD WOULD FIND THIS PERSON TRYING TO REACH OUT AND FORM HIS OWN SOCIETY OR FAMILY, FOR MANY TIMES IT IS BETWEEN THE 21st AND 28th YEAR THAT PEOPLE BECOME MARRIED OR ENTANGLED WITH THE PRODUCING OF CHILDREN.

YOU WILL FIND THAT IN THE YEARS FROM 28 TO 35 THEIR REACHING OUT IS A SETTLING DOWN AND FINDING THEIR OWN STABILITY, THEIR FAMILY WORTH, REACHING FOR

KNOWLEDGE THAT CAN BE HELPFUL AND BENEFICIAL TO ALL WITHIN THEIR OWN CONFINES.

THE NEXT PERIOD WOULD FIND THEM AGAIN REACHING OUTWARD TOWARD A MORE SATISFACTUAL SPIRITUAL EXPERIENCE, ONE IN WHICH THEY CAN IDENTIFY THEMSELVES WITH THE WORLD. THIS WOULD BE WHEN MOST PEOPLE WOULD BE AT THEIR TIME OF HELPING OR TEACHING OTHERS, MOVING INTO A LIFETIME WORK WITH A MEANING.

FROM 42 ON, YOU WILL FIND THE MOST SPIRITUAL ASPECTS OF ONE WHO IS ON A POSITIVE CYCLE IN THIS LIFETIME. YOU WILL ALSO FIND THAT THIS MARKS A POINT WHEN MANY WHO ARE NOT ON A SPIRITUAL PATH WILL BEGIN TO FALL AWAY OR DISINTEGRATE OR DECAY. THIS IS NOT A RAPID THING, BUT 42 IS USUALLY A CHANGING POINT IN LIFE.

LH It seems to come out like a Y, like it's all been fairly equal up to this time and then they either go up or go down.

S   THE OTHER CYCLES WITHIN A LIFE ARE MERGINGS WITH PEOPLE. YOU WILL FIND THAT THESE ARE GREATLY AFFECTED BY THE MOON AND THE STARS, THOSE WHICH ARE IN IMPORTANT POSITIONS WITHIN THAT PERSON'S HOROSCOPE.

LH Or systems . . . I can't get the word . . . but it has something to do with solar.

S   THESE ARE VARYING ACCORDING TO THE PERSON'S OWN ABILITIES. THIS IS NOT AS MUCH ACCORDING TO THEIR POSITIVE AND NEGATIVE ASPECTS AS TO THEIR INTENSITY, FOR THOSE WHO ARE VERY INTENSE WILL FIND THAT THEY HAVE THE HIGHEST AND LOWEST OF MOODS, WHILE OTHERS WHO ARE NOT QUITE AS INTENSE HAVE A MUCH MORE EVEN DISPOSITION. THESE ARE USUALLY THE ANALYTICAL OR CLINICAL PEOPLE.

LH Somehow artists seem to fall more into the mood swings. Of course, I know there are more than just artists, but that represents a group. Now, the nation seems to go more like waves or breakers, rather than in cycles or around.

PB Why does competition seem to be so much a part of human life?

S   IT IS BECAUSE OF THIS TRAIT THAT MUCH PROGRESS IS MADE. IT IS BECAUSE IT STIRS FORTH THE MOTIVATION WITHIN ONE SOUL AND ANOTHER TO COMPETE, OR TO BECOME BETTER THAN THAT WHICH THEY ARE, OR THAT WHICH THEY SEE. THIS IS A NECESSARY ELEMENT. HOWEVER IT IS ONE WHICH MUST BE USED WITH GREAT CAUTION, FOR THE EGO CAN ALSO BE GREATLY ENHANCED BY THIS FEELING OF COMPETITION.

LH And it feels as though it's to be used for growth and not for ego.

PB In other words, it's necessary for spiritual growth?

S   RIGHT.

PB Do other life forms all compete within their own form as well as with other forms?

S   NO, NOT ALL OTHER FORMS OF LIFE . . .

LH And they capitalize that "Life" for some reason.

S   NOT ALL OTHER FORMS OF LIFE ARE COMPETITIVE, FOR WHEN ONE HAS LEARNED TO MOTIVATE HIMSELF PROPERLY, OR TO BE THAT WHICH HE IS, TO BE WITH THE ONE AND ALL . . .

LH And those are both capitalized.

S   . . . IT IS NOT NECESSARY TO COMPETE, FOR HE HAS FOUND HIS PATH AND THE WAY IN WHICH HE MUST TRAVEL. AND HE KNOWS HIS NEED TO MOVE ONWARD ON HIS OWN.

LH But that seems to be a life form that's beyond the earth, not before coming to earth.

PB Will man compete in space as he has in the tribal form and in nationalism?

S   YES. THERE WILL BE A MEASURED AMOUNT OF COOPERATION
     AMONG MEN ON THIS TRIP, BUT THERE IS STILL THE COMPETI-
     TION FEELING, AND WARS MAY COME BECAUSE OF IT.

PB   Is this a part of the overall plan?

S   COMPETITIVENESS IS A PART OF THE GROWTH CYCLE AND
     VERY NECESSARY. THE TRIP INTO SPACE IS SOMETHING THAT
     WILL BE A PART OF THE FUTURE WORLD. IT, TOO, IS
     NECESSARY, FOR AS MAN BEGINS TO REACH OUT BEYOND HIS
     OWN PLANET, HE WILL RECOGNIZE THE GREATER FORCES
     THAT ARE THERE. IT WILL LIFT HIM UP OUT OF THE MIRE, SO
     TO SPEAK.

PB   Is there an opposing force?

S   THERE IS A FORCE WHICH IS CALLED EVIL. BY MANY IT IS
     CALLED DEVIL. BY OTHERS IT IS CALLED NEGATIVISM. THIS
     IS A FORCE WHICH CAN BE TURNED INTO POSITIVE ENERGY. IT
     IS NOT SOMETHING WHICH IS POWERFUL IN ITSELF, BUT IS
     RATHER A FORCE OR AN IMPELLING THING.

PB   Can we, by thinking positively and rightly, change that
     opposing force to a positive force for ourselves?

S   YOU PUT UP A BARRIER OF ENERGY AROUND YOURSELF AND IT
     IS BY DOING THIS THAT YOU ARE THEN MORE ABLE TO COPE
     WITH THE HIGHER THINGS WHICH COME TO YOU AND THUS
     YOU MAKE YOUR CHOICE. YOU ARE NOT LUKEWARM. YOU
     USE THIS ENERGY THAT IS LIKE THE BARRIER. YOU TURN IT
     INTO AN ACTIVE FORCE. YES.

PB   Many people seem to be fearful of being handled by the
     devil, this negative force. Is this a real danger?

S   THEY NEED TO RE-EXAMINE THE DEEPER THOUGHTS THAT ARE
     WITHIN THEMSELVES, BECAUSE THROUGH THIS FEAR THEY
     ARE DRAWING THAT TO THEM. MANY TIMES THEY HAVE
     VERY UNWORTHY THOUGHTS WITHIN AND THIS CAUSES THEM
     TO HOPE. . . .

LH And it's like a torn feeling . . . almost like they hope this will be their excuse.

S   YES, IT IS POSSIBLE TO OPEN THE BARRIER EVEN BY THE FEAR THAT IS GIVEN OFF, BECAUSE FEAR IN ITSELF IS AN ENERGY. THIS NEEDS TO BE RE-DIRECTED.

PB I don't have this fear. Am I under a false illusion about the clarity of my thought, or am I clear enough not to have to be concerned by it?

LH I don't feel . . . ah . . . all right. It says YOU ARE ALL RIGHT. And from you I feel a force field go out . . . like it can't come in because you are keeping it outgoing. It's not because you are fighting that, in particular, or worrying about it, or trying to convert the energy, but it's almost like you are protected by a force field.

PB Is this force field from outside myself?

S   FROM WITHIN.

LH It seems to go out from the inner. Now, if you had fear, I could feel a crack in that. Or if you were angry, or all these different things. You may have these really within you, but apparently they are not strong enough to break this force field.

PB How does one raise one's vibration level for protection?

LH Instead of being so aware of other people and wholeness and beauty and all this, it feels as though you're guarded in your thinking. And I keep getting the word "NEGATIVE, NEGATIVE, NEGATIVE" as though people use negative thoughts or use negative things far more than they are aware of. And so this is where I get this "ON GUARD."

S   BE AWARE OF EVERYTHING THAT GOES THROUGH YOUR MIND AND EVALUATE IT UNTIL YOU ARE SURE THAT THE THINGS THAT GO THROUGH ARE NOT . . .

LH   Well, they don't seem to need to be guarded as much.
     The protection seems to start from a very physical or
     disciplined way. Even though I always tell people all
     they have to do is picture light, so I guess I'm wrong. Ex-
     cuse me.

PB   Will there always be an opposing force or co-existence?

S   UNTIL ALL BECOME PERFECT, YES.

PB   How best can one protect against this opposing force?

S   BY GUARDING ONE'S SELF AND ONE'S CONSCIOUS MIND ON A
     CONSISTENT AND CONSTANT BASIS; BY BEING TOTALLY
     AWARE OF EACH THOUGHT AS IT ENTERS YOUR OWN MIND; BY
     BEING TOTALLY AWARE OF THOSE PEOPLE WHO ARE AROUND
     YOU; BY ALIGNING YOURSELF WITH THE FORCES OF GOOD
     AND RIGHT; BY CONSTANTLY PLACING YOURSELF IN EVER-
     BETTER POSITIONS . . .

LH   And this seems to be in relation to the company you
     keep, the circles you move in.

PB   How can we differentiate between good and bad?

S   ONLY BY YOUR RATE OF PROGRESS WILL YOU BE ABLE TO DO
     THIS, FOR TO EACH AREA THAT A PERSON ENTERS HE WILL
     FIND THAT THE THINGS WHICH APPEARED TO BE GOOD BE-
     FORE, NOW APPEAR AS LESSER OR LOWER OR EVIL NOW. YOU
     WILL FIND THAT AS YOU PROGRESS THERE IS A CONSTANT
     WEEDING AWAY OF THINGS WHICH APPEARED TO BE GOOD BE-
     FORE. THIS IS JUST AN EVOLVING PROCESS. YOU MUST BE PA-
     TIENT WITH YOURSELF AND WITH OTHER PEOPLE. PROGRESS
     AS YOU ARE ABLE, KNOWING THAT THESE THINGS WHICH ARE
     RIGHT FOR YOU WILL EVER BE PLACED WITHIN YOUR PATH OR
     SCOPE.

PB   This seems to bring up the competition again. Why?

S   ONLY BY VIEWING YOURSELF IN REGARDS TO OTHERS, OR BY
     VIEWING CERTAIN PLANES OF LIFE IN REGARDS TO OTHERS,

ARE YOU ABLE TO COMPARE SO THAT YOU CAN SEE THE DIF-
FERENCE BETWEEN THE GREATER AND THE LESSER, THE BET-
TER AND THE POORER, THE HIGHER AND THE LOWER. THERE
MUST BE A RELATIVITY SO THAT JUDGEMENT CAN BE PER-
FORMED . . . JUDGMENT ONLY OF YOURSELF AND YOUR OWN
PROGRESS, NOT OF OTHERS, FOR EACH ONE HAS HIS OWN
PATH, HIS OWN RATE OF GROWTH, AND HIS OWN FREE WILL.

PB   How can we learn, we who are interested in these subjects, a more adequate language for discussing metaphysical matters?

S   IT WILL BE MOST NECESSARY TO BRING INTO PLAY THE AREA
OF FEELINGS SO THAT PEOPLE CAN FEEL YOUR MEANING AS
MUCH AS TO HEAR IT. WHEN ONE INTELLECTUALIZES TOO
COMPLETELY, IT IS DIFFICULT, FOR THEN THE SEMANTICS BE-
COME SO VERY, VERY FINE—OR DELICATE. IT IS EXTREMELY
DIFFICULT TO RELATE THESE THINGS IN A MATTER OF WORDS.
HOWEVER, CONTINUE TO TRY AND YOU WILL FIND THAT NEW
WORDS MUST BE COINED TO BRING ABOUT FINER MEANINGS.

LH   And I keep feeling the solar plexis as though this plays a
very important part in it, so that even though your
words may not be quite the same as someone else's, the
feeling will be; so that you will be able to agree on a new
word, or a new something which coincides with the
feeling.

PB   Is the young generation understanding this particularly
well? Are they progressing in this direction?

LH   Yes . . . The only thing I see in a mirror dimly is,
though it's still clouded, it's coming.

S   THEY ARE AWARE OF THE FACT THAT WORDS ARE NOT SUFFI-
CIENT. HOWEVER, THEY HAVE A TENDENCY TO DWELL TOO
MUCH ON JUST THE FEELING THEY RECEIVE AND NOT TRYING
TO COMMUNICATE THIS IN A VERBAL MANNER. BOTH FACETS
MUST BE CLARIFIED.

PB With whom can these things be discussed?

LH It feels like a one-to-one basis . . . or two or three gathered together. Anyway, it has a very small feeling. But there seem to be fifteen small ones like this before they come together. And each one seems to be working on slightly different areas. And then they seem to come together to share what they have learned. And then each small group seems to shift in position, taking on a new area of thinking or discussion.

PB If life and time are eternal, why do we seem to have a sense of pushing to learn?

S   WHY SPEND AN ETERNITY IN ONE REALM WHEN THERE ARE SO MANY OTHER PLACES TO VISIT? KNOW THAT THIS IS NOT THE END RESULT NOR THE ALL-GOOD. KNOW THAT THERE IS MUCH TO BE ACCOMPLISHED, MUCH TO LEARN, AND THIS IS THE INQUISITIVE GOD WITHIN THAT CAUSES YOU TO CONTINUE TO SEARCH ONWARD EVER.

CHAPTER 2

Outside Guidance

On the highway to San Jose, Peter and I discussed which people we knew would be interested in hearing these tapes. Among our friends we had no idea who would accept these ideas or even be interested. There was a great reluctance to share them with those who were part of organized religious groups in case this would in any way offend their beliefs or confuse them.

In the end, we decided to wait until we had finished the series to see how we were led about this. Surely our guidance would direct us to the ones who hungered as we ourselves did for these answers.

I came into Lenora's house with an outpouring of gratitude for her gift and its availability to us.

"We feel so fortunate that you are here for us and this research together."

Lenora has a shy way of ducking her head, at once girlish and appealing.

"I do what I can," she said, "I only hope it is right and helpful."

Peter was setting up his equipment, smiling at Lenora's modesty.

"Today," he announced, "I want to ask your Source about guides."

PB   Does each entity have a guide?

LH   I get the word "GUARDIAN ANGEL," but that seems to be like with-you-always, or all through this particular existence. Now, when you say "guide," I feel a come-and-go as though there is a guide, but these seem to keep shifting as the person grows or changes.

PB   In other words, we have one entity progressing through different levels or planes and at each plane he has a different guide?

LH   And they feel in groups, like two, three, four. One seems to be in charge. You might call it Sergeant. It also feels Master Teacher or Master Guide in charge of many, because then I have the feeling of hundreds under one master.

PB   This was to be the next question: Does each entity have a group of guides?

S   YES.

PB   Please describe in detail.

S   THE STRUCTURE OF THE SYSTEM IS NOT UNLIKE THAT UPON THE EARTH PLANE. YOU WILL FIND THAT THERE ARE AREAS WHERE THERE IS NEED FOR PEOPLE TO BE WITHIN HOSPITAL AREAS, SO THAT THEY MAY RECEIVE MORE DEDICATED HELP OR CARE. MORE ON A ONE-TO-ONE BASIS.

LH   And that seems to be like intensive care.

PB   Define what a guide or master is.

S   A GUIDE CAN BE ONE WHO IS DEEPLY INTERESTED IN A PAR-TICULAR ENTITY, OR HAS AN AFFINITY FOR THE TYPE OF

WORK THAT ENTITY IS TRYING TO ACCOMPLISH. A GUIDE IS ONE WHO CARES, WHO IS ALSO EVOLVING HIS OWN GROWTH AND IS LEARNING AND HELPING, AND, QUOTE, "EARNING POINTS BY HELPING OTHERS." IT IS ONE WHO HAS A TALENT OR ABILITY THAT CAN BE PASSED ON TO ANOTHER. THIS IS A TASK THAT IS ASSUMED WILLINGLY OR NOT AT ALL. ONE IS NOT ASSIGNED AGAINST HIS OWN VOLITION. A GUIDE USUAL-LY WORKS WITH A SMALLER GROUP, FOR HE DOES NOT HAVE THE POWER AND ENERGY TO BE ABLE TO WORK WITH MANY. THERE ARE GUIDES WHO WORK SPECIFICALLY WITH ONE PER-SON, OR ONE ENTITY, AND THERE ARE THOSE WHO WORK WITH AS MANY AS THREE. SOME EVEN WORK WITH AS MANY AS TEN.

A MASTER IS A MUCH HIGHER EVOLUTION OF A SOUL, ONE WHO DOES NOT NEED TO INCARNATE AGAIN ON THE EARTH PLANE, ONE WHO HAS WISDOM AND MORE DETACH-MENT, ONE WHO IS ABLE TO GIVE LOVINGLY, FREELY, WITH-OUT JUDGMENT, ONE WHO IS ABLE TO MORE CLEARLY SEE THE LESSONS AND HOW THEY CAN BE LEARNED FOR THE ENTITY'S GREATEST GOOD.

LH It almost feels like a guide and a master could be arguing as though the guide would say, "But I want to do it this way," and the master would say, "But that is not for his highest good." He feels like a supervisor.

PB Describe their level of existence.

LH It's saying "HAVE YOU EVER TRIED TO DRAW A PICTURE OF THE SUN'S RAYS?"

S HAVE YOU EVER TRIED TO DRAW A DROP OF WATER WITHIN THE STREAM OF MOVING WATER? HAVE YOU EVER TRIED TO DEFINE A PARTICLE OF AIR? THESE ARE EXTREMELY DIF-FICULT TO PUT INTO WORDS. HOWEVER, KNOW THAT THESE ARE SOMETHING OF WHICH YOU CAN BECOME CONSCIOUSLY AWARE AS YOU SEEK TO LEARN FOR YOURSELF. YOU WILL FIND THAT YOU CAN GO INTO MEDITATION AND LITERALLY SEE THESE REALMS OF EXISTENCE, AND YET THEY ARE NOT

SOMETHING WHICH YOU CAN PUT FENCES AROUND OR PUT
WORDS AROUND. EVEN THE DESCRIPTION IS MOST DIFFICULT.
YOU MIGHT SAY THAT THE GUIDES ARE OF A MORE VISIBLE
NATURE TO MANKIND THAN THE MASTERS. THE MASTERS
COME MORE AS A FEELING OR AN ESSENCE, WHILE THE
GUIDES STILL HAVE MORE OF A SPIRITUAL VAPOR OR BODY
ABOUT THEM.

THERE IS NOT SUCH A THING AS NIGHT AND DAY, NOR
TIME, WITH THESE, THUS THERE'S MORE INFINITE PATIENCE
THAN MANKIND HAS YET BEEN ABLE TO FIND. THERE IS STILL
A MEASURE OF EMOTION AND FEELING (OR BLOCKING) WITH
GUIDES, WHILE THOSE WHO HAVE BECOME MASTERS ARE
ABOVE AND BEYOND THIS STATE OF AWARENESS. THEY ARE
ABLE TO ALLOW THE FLOW WITHOUT BLOCKING ANYTHING OR
WITHOUT FEELING, AND YET THERE IS GREAT COMPASSION OR
GREAT UNDERSTANDING, BUT NOT PHYSICAL FEELING.

LH Guides seem to still have a certain amount of that.

PB I understand the Akashic Records record every pulsation,
every beat, or whatever. Is it only in this solar system
and what do they actually record?

S   THERE ARE OTHER RECORDS THAT RECORD FOR OTHER UNI-
VERSES. HOWEVER, ALL THAT HAS TAKEN PLACE WITHIN THIS
UNIVERSE SHOULD BE WITHIN THE AKASHIC RECORD IF ONE IS
ABLE TO TAP IT. YOU WILL FIND THIS CAN BE DONE. IT IS EX-
TREMELY ESSENTIAL THAT YOU GO THROUGH THE PROPER
CHANNEL AND MASTER, FOR NOT ALL ARE ABLE TO TAP INFI-
NITE KNOWLEDGE THAT IS THERE.

LH That doesn't seem right, but that's what I get.

PB The Akashic Records are of one universe. Is this
universe known to man or is it beyond the concept of
man's knowledge today?

S   MAN KNOWS OF THE OUTER AREAS OF THIS UNIVERSE, BUT HE
HAS NOT YET BEEN ABLE TO EXPLORE THEM EVEN WITH HIS

MOST DEVELOPED TELESCOPES OR VISUALIZING EQUIPMENT, BUT HE SEEMS TO KNOW ROUGHLY WHERE IT ENDS.

PB Are there entities whose sole function it is to read and interpret the Akashic Records?

S YES.

LH I'm getting a chief librarian. And if I were to line up all masters, it feels like there are only certain ones of these masters that can tap the higher ones who know all.

PB Then this comes from the master to the guide to the individual?

S RIGHT. OR FROM THE MASTER TO THE INDIVIDUAL, DEPENDING ON WHETHER THE PERSON IS TUNED TO THAT MASTER.

LH It doesn't always seem to need to come through a guide. This seems to be why they were saying "be careful of the channel you go through" as to whether you would get a total answer.

PB So the masters are more or less at one level while the guides could be at varying levels of progress?

S YES. THE GUIDES COULD BE IDENTIFIED MORE AS A HUMAN. I MEAN THAT IF YOU KNOW A HUMAN PERSON, YOU COULD IDENTIFY BETTER THE QUALITIES OF A GUIDE.

PB Have they been on the earth level as humans?

S YES, ALL HAVE AT ONE TIME OR ANOTHER. THOSE WHO ARE MASTERS NOW HAVE EVOLVED BEYOND THE NECESSITY OF THIS ANY LONGER, AND YET THERE IS STILL THE NEED WITH THEM, OR THE ABILITY WITH THEM TO BE ABLE TO GUIDE AND DIRECT. HOWEVER, EVEN THESE RETURN TO OTHER SPHERES THAT THEY MAY CONTINUE TO GROW AND LEARN IN THEIR OWN RIGHT.

PB Are they, in fact, people?

S   NOT PEOPLE AS ENTITIES, BUT HAVE BEEN PEOPLE AS CON-
SCIOUSNESSES.

LH That's very awkward.

PB Are they limited to our solar system and /or universe?

LH The masters don't seem to be because I see them free to
go.

PB Are they limited to a known, finite area?

LH Yes, only that finite area is larger than I can put a fence
around. Yes. It seems to have limits way out somewhere
and then there is something higher than they are.

PB In other words, they are limited to a known, finite area
which may be known to them but infinite to us?

S   RIGHT.

PB Describe the various levels of guides and masters. Are
there masters and master-guides?

LH There's something. . . . I can't get it. Master beings or
master beloved. Wait a minute. It's spelled BRAH. . . .
It's not like brotherhood. It's something above masters,
but it's like a fuller degree of master. And there again, it
feels like one of these is over a smaller number of masters, where one master could be over a thousand guides
or a hundred. It's a finer degree, but I can't get the
name.

PB Can you explain more of this structure and system?

S   THERE ARE THOSE WHO ARE WELL GIFTED IN CERTAIN AREAS
OF LIFE AND THEY WILL ATTACH THEMSELVES TO THOSE WHO
HAVE THE MAKINGS OF THESE SAME GIFTS WITHIN THEM-
SELVES, SUCH AS ART, MUSIC, BUSINESS, ETC. THIS IS EX-
TREMELY IMPORTANT NOT ONLY TO THE ONE WHO IS WALK-
ING THE EARTH BUT THE ONE WHO WOULD ACT AS HIS GUIDE,
FOR IT IS A LEARNING PROCESS FOR BOTH. BY THE GUIDE
HELPING HIM, HE IS THEN ABLE TO MANIFEST EVEN GREATER

GIFTS IN HIS NEXT INCARNATION. IT IS A DUAL OR TWO-WAY STREET. IT IS NOT A CASE OF ALL GIVING FROM EITHER SIDE. THERE ARE THOSE WHO WOULD PROGRESS FROM BEGINNING TEACHERS TO LATER TEACHERS. AND THIS IS NOTED BY THE COLOR OR CHANGE OF THEIR AURA. THROUGH THIS, AND THE QUICKNESS OF LEARNING, THEY ARE ABLE TO KNOW WHEN ONE PARTICULAR BEING IS READY TO PROGRESS TO ANOTHER GROUP OF TEACHERS.

THERE ARE TIMES ALSO WHEN ONE OF A PARTICULAR RELIGIOUS BACKGROUND WILL COME TO HELP ONE WHO IS NOT PARTICULARLY DRAWN TO, QUOTE, "RELIGION." IT IS BY THIS WAY THAT MAN CAN THEN EXPAND HIS OWN ABILITIES AND FACETS. IT IS EXTREMELY IMPORTANT THAT HE BE WELL-ROUNDED. IT IS NOT WELL TO BE TOO OUT OF BALANCE IN ANY ONE AREA. HOWEVER, THIS IS ALSO THE REASON FOR MANY, MANY LIVES, FOR THROUGH THIS HE HAS AN ETERNITY TO MAKE PROGRESS AND BECOME MORE ROUNDED. THERE ARE THOSE WHO ARE EXTREMISTS IN THEIR PARTICULAR PROFESSION, THOSE WHO SEEM TO KNOW ALL THERE IS TO KNOW ABOUT A CERTAIN SUBJECT.

PB   Don't we need these for our leaders?

S   TRUE.

PB   Are all guides on the spirit level?

S   NO, FOR MANY OF THE GUIDES THAT ARE IN SPIRIT ARE OF A MUCH MORE HIGHLY EVOLVED NATURE. MANY OF THE GUIDELINES AND GUIDES WHICH MAN ALSO USES ARE UPON THE EARTH AROUND HIM. THESE CAN BE IN THE FORM OF FRIENDS, TEACHERS, BOOKS, ETC. THOSE WHO ARE STRICTLY UPON THE SPIRIT LEVEL ARE THOSE WHO ARE MORE SPECIALIZED OR ABLE TO HELP ONLY IN SPECIFIED AREAS.

LH   These are the ones who are more tied to earth. If they are good businessmen, they can give good business advice, but then they seem to be able to progress through that to a higher level. . . . I see the word "ECUMENICAL."

PB   Do all guides function as such to help humans?

S   INSOFAR AS THEY ARE ABLE TO CONCEIVE OF RIGHT, YES.
     THERE ARE MANY WHO ARE MISGUIDED. THE GUIDE IS NOT
     TRYING TO MISGUIDE OR MISLEAD, BUT IT IS A LACK OF
     KNOWLEDGE ON HIS PART.

PB   Does this lead to confusion and damage to their
     followers or disciples?

S   MANY BRING CONFUSION. THERE IS ALSO THE PROBLEM OF
     MISINTERPRETATION AS IT COMES THROUGH TO THOSE WHO
     ARE YET ON THE EARTH PLANE. THEY ARE NOT ABLE TO
     DEFINE THE FACT THAT THESE WHO HAVE PASSED ON ARE
     MANY TIMES SPEAKING FROM THEIR OWN EXPERIENCE. THIS
     EXPERIENCE MAY NOT HAVE ENDED IN A FRUITFUL VENTURE.

PB   How can one tell?

S   ONLY BY LISTENING TO THE GUIDANCE WHICH COMES
     THROUGH AND WEIGHING IT IN THE LIGHT OF TODAY'S PROB-
     LEMS, TODAY'S KNOWING. KNOW THAT YOU USE THIS STRICT-
     LY AS GUIDANCE AND NOT AS GOSPEL TRUTH OR LAW. THEN
     YOU ARE ON FIRM GROUND. KNOW THAT THESE EXPERIENCES
     CAN BE HELPFUL TO YOU EVEN AS THOSE AROUND YOU ON
     EARTH CAN BE BENEFICIAL. GAIN BY OTHERS' KNOWLEDGE,
     GAIN BY THEIR EXPERIENCE, BUT DO NOT RELY ON IT
     TOTALLY.

PB   Does Universal Mind prompt or prod individuals in cer-
     tain directions?

S   YES. IT IS THE MOTIVATING FORCE. IT IS THAT DESIRE
     WITHIN MAN WHICH CAUSES HIM TO FEEL RESTLESS AND
     GIVES HIM THE KNOWING THAT THERE ARE OTHER THINGS HE
     NEEDS TO BE DOING. HOWEVER, THIS IS WHERE FREE WILL
     COMES IN, AND IT MAY BE DENIED.

PB   Does the individual's guide or master do this for Univer-
     sal Mind or in addition to Universal Mind?

S IN MOST CASES THE MASTERS OR GUIDES ARE THOSE WHICH ARE THE CHANNELS TO AN INDIVIDUAL ON THE EARTH PLANE. HOWEVER, THE TOTAL PROMPTING CAN COME THROUGH MANY SOURCES. IT CAN COME AS FRIENDS OR RELATIVES, TEACHERS, OR THOSE WHO WOULD ENCOURAGE EVEN FROM THE PHYSICAL PLANE. IT CAN ALSO COME IN THE FORM OF BOOKS. BUT THE ACTUAL PROMPTING COMES FROM SPIRIT OR ENERGY BEYOND.

LH Now, if these don't make sense, let me know, because I can't tell sometimes whether it's . . .

PB I'd rather not think about it now. I'm asking through you and you're answering through or from Universal Mind.

LH I'm staying out of it as much as I can.

PB And I'm not thinking about the answers either.

LH Very good.

PB So I want to stay out of it too.

LH Fine.

PB Are suggestions sometimes placed in an individual's subconscious unbeknownst to him?

S YES, AND THIS AGAIN CAN COME FROM MANY SOURCES. IT CAN COME FROM THE ETHER OR THE AIR ABOUT A PERSON, COMING FROM OTHER THOUGHT . . .

LH IT SAYS "THOUGHT FORMS." All right . . .

S . . . OTHER THOUGHT FORMS WHICH ARE DWELLING IN THE AIR, THESE BEING FROM BOTH THE PHYSICAL PLANE AND THE ETHERIC PLANE. THE THOUGHTS CAN ALSO BE CONSCIOUSLY PLACED THERE BY THOSE WHO ARE AROUND THE PERSON IN A PHYSICAL FORM. THEY ARE PLACED THERE MANY TIMES UNCONSCIOUSLY BY ELDERS AND PLAYMATES IN THE EARLIER

PART OF LIFE. THE MIND IS A TREMENDOUS RESERVOIR WHICH STORES ALL THINGS THAT COME TO IT. IT DOES NOT RATIONALIZE NOR FIGURE THOSE THINGS WHICH ARE COMING IN, BUT DOES STORE THEM IN THIS RESERVOIR.

PB Define intelligence.

S   INTELLIGENCE MAY ALSO BE CALLED UNDER THE MISNOMER, NATURE. INTELLIGENCE IS THE INNATE KNOWING OF THAT WHICH MUST BE, SUCH AS THE GENES WITHIN THE BODY WHICH CAUSE A CERTAIN CHARACTERISTIC TO BE MADE MANIFEST. THIS IS INTELLIGENCE. INTELLIGENCE IS NOT NECESSARILY A SCHOOLING OR CREATING OF MIND TO A DEGREE THAT MIND CAN EXHIBIT INTELLIGENCE.

PB When one recognizes a problem and lifts it to Universal Mind, is the entity actually being helped directly by Universal Mind or by one of the masters or guides?

S   AGAIN NO PAT ANSWER HERE. THERE ARE TIMES WHEN THERE ARE GUIDES OR HELPERS ON THE OTHER SIDE THAT CAN BE OF MORE DIRECT HELP OR INFLUENCE UPON THE SITUATION AROUND THAT ENTITY THAN CAN THE . . .

LH It uses the term "NEBULOUS FORCE OF UNIVERSAL MIND."

S   . . . HOWEVER, AS THE UNIVERSAL MIND CONSCIOUSNESS WITHIN THAT ENTITY IS ABLE TO RISE TO A HIGHER DEGREE, HE CAN THEN BE HELPED MORE DIRECTLY BY UNIVERSAL MIND THAN THROUGH THE AID OF HELPERS.

PB Is this one reason why an entity seems to be clearer than at other times?

S   ONE IS AT HIS CLEAREST WHEN HE IS ABLE TO MAKE THE DIRECT CONTACT. WHEN HE NEEDS THE HELP OF OUTSIDE GUIDING INFLUENCES, HE IS ALSO INFLUENCED BY THAT ONE'S OWN PROGRESS AND FREE WILL.

LH It's like a shadow . . . or shade . . . shadings.

PB Then this means that not only the clarity of the channel or master is involved?

S AMEN.

PB How can I get so that I can communicate with my guide at will?

LH I see you with a great big fancy ham set, the radio amateur set, with all the knobs and dials that you are turning. Just a moment. Well, it says . . .

S IN THE SILENCE OF YOUR MEDITATION YOU WILL FIND THAT YOU ARE ABLE TO DO THIS.

LH And you seem to be well aware of the difference of 'I thought' or 'it comes to me.'

PB That's true. It has come to me, and now it doesn't, and I wonder why shouldn't I be able to communicate any time, anywhere, at will?

LH You should. It says:

S YOU SHOULD BE ABLE TO DO THIS AT ALL TIMES WHEN YOU ARE IN THE PROPER FRAME OF MIND. YOU WILL FIND THAT EVEN WHEN YOU ARE IN A DEPRESSED MOOD, THIS SHOULD NOT BE SOMETHING WHICH CAUSES YOU TO BE LACKING IN HELP. CONTINUE TO SEEK, AND DO NOT DROP AWAY FROM THIS. PRACTICE MAKES PERFECT.

(Peter's questions triggered some of my own.)

JB Explain about the same guardian angel being with you always. (All my life I have felt this presence.)

S THIS GUARDIAN ANGEL WITH YOU ALWAYS IN THIS LIFETIME IS SOMEONE WHO HAS EVOLVED VERY HIGHLY AND IS VERY ATTUNED TO YOU. THEY FEEL EMOTIONALLY WHAT YOU FEEL, AND ALTHOUGH THEY DO NOT KNOW ALL THE WAYS TO HELP, THEY KNOW WHERE TO GET HELP.

JB   Are you a guide or Master, and do you have a special name to identify you by?

S   I HAVE BEEN A GUIDE FOR MANY ENTITIES AND HAVE BEEN A MASTER MANY TIMES. NOW I AM CALLED MASTER OF MIND BY THE ONE I AM UNDER, ALTHOUGH I HAVE HAD MANY NAMES. IT IS NOT IMPORTANT TO KNOW WHO I AM, ONLY THAT YOU HAVE HELP WHEN YOU NEED IT. ALWAYS ASK FOR THE HIGHEST BEING IN YOUR QUESTIONING OR SEARCHING. IT IS IMPORTANT. TIME MEANS NOTHING TO ME.

JB   Why are so many couples being separated?

S   THEY ARE BEING SEPARATED TO DEVELOP THEIR OWN INDIVIDUALITY AND TO LEARN THEIR SEPARATE LESSONS. IT IS ALL FOR A PURPOSE.

JB   Why are children's lives being so fractured?

S   THIS IS HAPPENING RIGHT NOW IN YOUR SOCIETY BECAUSE THEY ARE ENTITIES WHO HAVE CAUSED DISTURBANCES IN FORMER LIFETIMES AND BECAUSE THEY NOW HAVE AVAILABLE TO THEM THE HELP OF HYPNOSIS AND PSYCHOLOGY AND DO NOT NEED THE FORMER NURTURING OF TWO PARENTS AND A SOLID FAMILY. THEY ARE BEING TAUGHT LESSONS FOR THE FUTURE WORLD THEY ARE TO ADAPT TO.

JB   What lessons must I consider for my future?

S   YOU MUST LEARN TO BE MORE DECISIVE AND MORE INDEPENDENT. YOU MUST LEARN TO FEEL COMPASSION FOR EMOTIONAL INVOLVEMENTS AROUND YOU WITHOUT BEING PULLED INTO IT.

JB   Should I further explore the Eastern religions or stay with Christianity for my inner guidance?

S   YOU ALREADY HAVE A GOOD BALANCED KNOWLEDGE OF THE LESSONS OF CHRISTIANITY AND ARE NOT TIED TO ONLY THAT AREA OF RELIGION, BECAUSE YOU CAN REACH OUT AND TAKE

BITS AND PIECES FROM OTHER RELIGIONS AND INTEGRATE
THEM INTO WHAT YOU KNOW AND NEED.

JB   Should I cut down my sleeping hours, or am I getting
guidance during these hours?

S   WAKE UP EARLY IN THE MORNING FOR MEDITATION WHERE
YOU WILL BE ADVISED AND GUIDED.

It is of interest to note that I turned to my guides for help
with the transcribing and collating here. Each time before sitting down to work, I asked that someone stand by to assure
the accuracy and determine what segments should be in-
cluded. Although I had considered all personal information
inappropriate to this more abstract work, at the completion
of the first draft I consulted with Lenora's Source to be told
that the manuscript "SHOULD BE EXPANDED IN A MORE PERSONAL
WAY TO MAKE IT MORE READABLE."

Whenever I found myself making typing errors, I knew
that it was a message, so I stopped to "listen." Sometimes it
meant a word was missing, or the answer was duplicated on
a former page, but always it was a signal for my attention.
This exercise alerted me to the assistance available in other
decisions of my life.

To my question of what was to become of this venture,
Lenora was shown an upside-down umbrella—a straight line
with many spokes—saying that "multiple things come out of
it," also that I would meet the people to expedite the next
step when my part was finished.

Meditation, when I first awoke at 5:30 each day, became
a practice.

CHAPTER 3

Reincarnation

Lenora was looking fresh, rested and unhurried.

"We should have a particularly good session today," said Peter. "This part will include questions on reincarnation."

"You ask the questions and I'll do what I can," answered Lenora. "So far I've found it all interesting. I just wish I could recall it all."

"How could you when we've covered so much ground?"

Once again we were seated at her same diningroom table, feeling very at home in our accustomed places.

Lenora was both earnest and businesslike about our sessions, never stopping for a break or anything to eat or to drink. She picked up her pen as he started his tape recorder.

PB   Are we really completely spiritual, mental beings?

S   THIS IS THE FORCE OR POWER WITHIN THAT WHICH IS CALLED MAN. THE PHYSICAL PART, OR EVIDENCE THAT IS SEEN, IS A VERY REAL PART IN THAT IT CAN CAUSE MUCH OF THE . . .

LH   It says "DETERRING" . . .

S   . . . DETERRING FACTORS IN MAN'S GROWTH. HOWEVER, THE SPIRITUAL IS THE TRUE OR ONGOING PART. THIS IS THE EVIDENCE WHICH OCCURS FROM LIFE TO LIFE.

PB Do we live lives on other planets or worlds?

S Yes. However, this is in a matter of eons, and not in earth years as you recognize them. It is a period of many, many lifetimes of evolution from one realm to another.

LH The only kind of thing I'm getting as far as numbers is like one . . . zero . . . zero . . . six zeros . . . and this is not old.

PB Do other types of beings exist in space also, or in other worlds?

LH As you first started to talk I got yes.

S Yes, there are many which would be recognizable to you and many which would not be recognizable, for their form is so completely different from that which you recognize. But even at that, they have a mentality of form.

LH And some feel below and some feel above or beyond us, but the body I am seeing, or the form, is completely different than anything I could recognize. Some of them look more like a glob. (laugh)

PB Do various beings have areas of operation in the universe?

S There is an overlapping of universe forms. There is an area where many of these of lower vibration come to you for growth and protection, for loving and learning. There are also those of higher realms who come back to aid and abet those who are yet on this plane.

PB Is the universe, as we know it, all there is?

S No. There is an infinite amount of knowledge that man has yet to tap. Much of it is beyond his comprehension until he increases his vocabulary or men-

TAL AWARENESS. TO EACH IS GIVEN THAT WHICH HE CAN
HANDLE AT THE MOMENT.

LH But it seems to go way, way, way, way beyond anything I can reach.

PB I think of a story of beings who are able to travel in
space and on various worlds. And these beings grew
everything such as houses, vehicles, space ships, and so
on, rather than converting and moulding matter. Now,
the question is: Does man grow the body as a vehicle?

S MAN CONCEIVES THE IDEA AND THUS IS ABLE TO CREATE
FROM THAT. THE OTHER BEINGS ARE THOSE WHICH CAN
CREATE BY MENTAL IMAGE, AND THUS CAUSE IT TO MANIFEST
IN WHAT APPEARS TO BE SPACE. ALL THE MATERIALS OR IONS
ARE WITHIN THE ATMOSPHERE ABOVE THEM. IT IS JUST A
MATTER OF CONVERSION.

PB Must we reach a pure, spiritual plane to learn to understand and control time?

S THIS CAN BE REACHED BEFORE A MATTER OF COMPLETE MEN-
TAL PURITY. HOWEVER, THE MORE PURENESS THAT IS MANI-
FEST, THE MORE NEARLY MAN WILL BE ABLE TO CONTROL
EVEN HIS OWN TIME AND HIS OWN SELF.

LH It feels like the universes . . . I don't know what to call
it, because I don't have the right words . . . but in the
progression beyond this planet, there doesn't seem to be
time.

PB Since individuals have free will, is it reasonable to
assume that their destinies are not pre-set?

S IT IS ONLY THAT THE TIMING IS NOT PRE-SET. THERE ARE
CERTAIN TASKS WHICH HAVE BEEN SET FOR EACH SOUL TO AC-
COMPLISH IN A GIVEN LIFETIME. HOWEVER, THIS IS NOT A
HARD AND FIRM RULE. IF THAT SOUL SO CHOOSES, IT MAY

TAKE SEVERAL LIFETIMES TO ACCOMPLISH THESE SAME THINGS. DO NOT FEEL THAT THERE IS A SET TIME OR PUNISHMENT FOR LACK OF COOPERATION. THIS IS WHERE FREE WILL ENTERS IN, THAT EACH ONE CAN MOVE AT A GIVEN SPEED.

PB Frequently a person seems to need what another has to offer, such as love, inspiration, approval, encouragement, and so on. If the person who could supply the other's need fails to do so, will the needy one fulfill his need with someone else or in another way?

S THE NEED WILL BE FULFILLED. HOWEVER, NOT ALWAYS IN ONE GIVEN LIFETIME, AS WAS STATED BEFORE. IT IS NECESSARY THAT CERTAIN SOULS HAVE EACH OF THESE QUALITIES SO THAT THEY MAY BECOME MORE ROUNDED. THIS IS THE CAUSE OF MANY SOUL HURTS FROM LIFETIME TO LIFETIME: THE LACK OF LOVE, THE LACK OF UNDERSTANDING, THE LACK OF ACCEPTANCE. MANY OF THESE THINGS CAUSE A DEEP AND UNERRING . . .

LH I don't think that fits in there, but that's the word.

S . . . UNERRING HURTS TO ONE. YES, THERE IS MORE THAN A SINGLE CHANNEL THROUGH WHICH THESE NEEDS MAY BE FULFILLED. IT CAN COME IN VARYING WAYS.

PB Was man put on earth or did he evolve?

S MAN, AS BODY, HAS EVOLVED. HOWEVER, MAN AS SPIRIT WAS PLACED UPON THE EARTH THROUGH CHOICE. IT WAS A COMING OF THE SOUL INTO THAT BODY WHICH WAS ALREADY PLACED THERE AS A MATERIAL OR ANIMAL BEING. THIS IS NOT TO SAY THAT MIND OR SOUL ENTERED AN ANIMAL BODY, BUT THAT IT CHOSE THIS VEHICLE AS A METHOD OF EXPRESSION.

PB Was life started, then, on earth with a general evolutionary plan?

S MANY FORMS OF ANIMAL BEINGS HAVE EVOLVED UPON THE FACE OF THE EARTH AND THIS WAS LONG BEFORE MAN, AS SUCH, CAME TO THE EARTH—MAN AS MIND OR SPIRIT.

LH There seem to be two separate things, and I can see algae and so forth and so on, and it seems to progress, progress, and then man or spirit seems to come down. Ah . . . I use the term 'come down from above' but it's like a meeting at a certain place rather than saying that mind kept expanding or evolving.

PB In other words, there seems to have been a time or balance with which man's level of spiritual existence was not in harmony with the earth and then it was?

LH I don't feel harmony as much as challenge. As though this body is now ready for spirit, and spirit descends or enters in and uses this as a challenge to make further growth.

PB What is spirit?

S   SPIRIT IS A WORD THAT IS MANY TIMES USED INTER-CHANGEABLY WITH SOUL. HOWEVER, SPIRIT IS THE LOWER FORM OF SOUL, SOUL BEING THE ONGOING PART OF ALL THAT IS. SPIRIT IS THE PART OR THE ESSENCE OF MAN AND IS YET SOMEWHAT ENCOMPASSED BY THE FEARS, FRUSTRATIONS, FALLACIES, EARTHINESS OF MAN. SPIRIT IS NOT YET THE PURE ESSENCE OF BEING SUCH AS SOUL.

PB Please define soul.

(Lenora looked at him with a startled expression. "That must be a high word," she said.)

S   SOUL IS THE ALL IN ALL. IT IS THAT WHICH IS GOD IN MAN. IT IS THAT WHICH IS ONGOING TOWARD ONENESS WITH GOD.

(She clarified further:)

LH It is a bit of the mass, and Mass seems to be a capital M. That's all.

PB Was earth manifested for man by man?

S THE EARTH, AS SUCH, WAS MANIFESTED OR MADE POSSIBLE
BY MIND . . .

LH And that's a capital M.

S . . . AND YET IT WAS FOR THE GROWTH OR POSSIBILITY OF
MIND WITHIN MAN. IT IS A GROWING PLACE. IT IS MADE TO
BECOME THE SERVANT OF MAN IF HE WILL UTILIZE IT PROPER-
LY. IT CAN BE INCREASED AND PERFECTED UNDER HIS DIREC-
TION AND CARE.

PB Is the earth manifested for other life forms as well?

S THERE ARE SEVERAL SPHERES OF GROWTH UPON THE EARTH,
MANY OF WHICH ARE NOT VISIBLE OR OF WHICH MAN IS NOT
AWARE. IT IS TO BE USED BY ALL AS THEIR NEED ARISES.

PB What, in fact, is progress?

S PROGRESS IS THE RETURNING TO THE ALL-IN-ALL OR THE
ONE-IN-ALL. IT IS THE RETURNING TO THE UNIVERSAL CON-
SCIOUSNESS FOR ALL SOULS. IT IS THE POOLING OF ABILITIES
AND CAPABILITIES OF RESOURCES BOTH PHYSICAL AND MEN-
TAL AND SPIRITUAL. IT IS THE COMPLETENESS OF ANY BEING.
PROGRESS IS PERFECTION.

PB Is all life and intelligence one?

S YES, THOUGH SELDOM RECOGNIZED.

PB Are beings truly self-governing at the higher levels?

S NOT ON AN INDIVIDUAL BASIS, FOR AS THEY REACH THE
HIGHER LEVELS, THERE IS MORE OF A COMMUNAL GOVERN-
ING OR A GOVERNING BY GENERAL CONSENT, SO THAT IT IS
NOT AN INDIVIDUAL THING OR AN I-AM-MY-OWN LAW.

PB Do we incarnate into other life beings here on earth?

S NOT ON THE EARTH PLANE IN A FORM OTHER THAN THAT
WHICH YOU RECOGNIZE AS HUMAN, BUT THERE ARE OTHER

AREAS OF INCARNATION IN OTHER REALMS OF REALITY SUCH
AS YOU HAVE WITNESSED IN THE DREAM STATE.

LH It feels like you have . . . I can't say 'astrally
travelled' . . . but as though you have witnessed other
forms in your dream state that . . . and some of it feels
like it's within our universe, and some of it feels like it's
beyond. Now, I don't know just what 'universe' in-
cludes. Maybe they are trying to say 'galaxy', but I keep
getting the word 'UNIVERSE' . . . and some of it feels
beyond that.

PB Define and describe astral travel.

S THIS IS THE RELEASING OF THE SPIRIT BODY FROM THE
PHYSICAL BODY SO THAT IT IS ABLE TO BE THE FREE SOUL
THAT IT NEEDS TO BE, OR THE FREE ENTITY THAT IT NEEDS TO
BE. HOWEVER, IT SHOULD NOT BE TOTALLY RELEASED FROM
THE BODY, NOR DONE AT INDISCRIMINATE WILL, FOR THIS
CAN BE A DANGEROUS PRACTICE. KNOW THAT IT CAN OCCUR
FOR BENEFICIAL PURPOSES, SUCH AS PURPOSES OF STUDY IN
THE ASTRAL REALM, OR PURPOSES OF HEALING, BUT TO USE
THIS AS A METHOD OF PLAY OR FUN IS NOT WELL, FOR IT
DOES DETRACT FROM THE ENERGY THAT IS WITHIN THE BODY.

LH And this seems to be the astral body or the spirit body,
not the physical body.

S IT CAN BE VERY DANGEROUS TO SOME WHO WOULD CHOOSE
TO USE THIS AS A MEANS TO ESCAPE FROM LIFE THAT IS
NECESSARY. IT CAN BE A GROWING EXPERIENCE. THERE IS
ALWAYS A FINE ATTACHMENT WHICH CAUSES THIS BODY TO
RETURN TO THE PHYSICAL SO THAT UNTIL ONE IS READY TO
LEAVE THE BODY PERMANENTLY, SUCH AS IN DEATH, ONE IS
ALWAYS ABLE TO RE-ENTER. HOWEVER, THE CORD OR ATTACH-
MENT MUST NOT BE BROKEN. THIS WOULD BE THE CASE MANY
TIMES WHEN PEOPLE ARE INSTITUTIONALIZED AS INSANE.
THEY HAVE MADE THESE ASTRAL TRIPS AND HAVE DESIRED
NOT TO RETURN TO THE BODY AND YET THE PHYSICAL IS STILL

AN ONGOING VEHICLE. THIS COULD BE BENEFITED IF THERE WERE ONE WHO COULD DRAW THIS ENTITY BACK INTO THE BODY AND CAUSE HIM TO TAKE UP THE REINS OF HIS WORK AGAIN AND CAUSE HIM TO MOVE FORWARD.

PB Thank you. Do inanimate objects have an intelligent life?

S ONLY AS THE LIFE IS WITHIN THE ATOMS THAT COMPOSE THAT INANIMATE OBJECT, BUT NOT AS A MIND OF THINKING AND PLANNING SUCH AS MAN ENTAILS.

PB Is there an orderly system of progress? For example, from inanimate objects to plants to insects to animals etc.?

S YES, TO THE SCOPE WITHIN WHICH THAT MATTER IS ALREADY ACCUSTOMED, BUT NOT INTO OTHER REALMS OF CONSCIOUSNESS.

PB There are other realms of consciousness?

LH Apparently. Who in the world am I to reel off these things to you, because I don't know. I haven't the slightest idea.

PB Well, *I* know, the less you think about these questions the better, because if you're surprised by the question or answer, sometimes it brings you out of whatever communicative state . . .

LH Well, I'm always aware of what's being said, but I don't know if it's complete or not. The only thing is that the *me* of me every once in a while says, 'How dare you sit there and let answers come through when you don't know whether they are right or wrong, but they flow through. O.K. Just so you understand how *I* feel.

PB I'll inject a question here for your Source. Would the answer flow through if it were improper for the person asking to have that answer?

LH It says "NO".

PB In other words, you are not going to ask any questions it wouldn't be right for you to answer.

LH Oh . . . O.K.

PB I sense this very clearly.

LH Hm-m-m.

PB Because you are drawing from Universal Mind. Now, why would Universal Mind put through you information that might be damaging or harmful to anyone?

LH Well, I guess in the beginning when people asked questions (and this still happens) . . . I thought, 'Now what if this doesn't all back each other up?' You know . . . what if this answer. . . . Oh, I shouldn't have brought this up, I guess. I just wanted you to know how sometimes I think, 'Boy, have I flipped!'

PB Now, I think this is well worth discussing. Let me ask you something. If you find yourself in a situation where you see certain things that other people don't see, do you volunteer to tell them what you are seeing if they don't ask you?

LH No.

PB Well, this is exactly the point. The person has to be seeking. And then the person really would get the information that he is entitled to at his present level of growth. Do you see what I mean?

LH Yes. O.K.

PB For example, if I were to give these same questions to some other person, it might very well be that they wouldn't come through you at all.

LH Oh. . . . But if you were to direct these questions to a different channel, I'd say you *should* get the same answers . . . if they are coming from Universal Intelligence. Right?

PB The answers would be very much the same.

LH Well, this is what I wonder sometimes, although I'm not interjecting anything. It still flows through. And I'm hopeful that these things can be proven sometime. That's all that worries me.

PB I don't think you should be concerned. Nothing is going to come through that you shouldn't have, or that the person asking shouldn't have.

LH All right. I used to worry about authority a great deal. I was always looking for an authority for anything *I* said. Well, I don't *have* an authority on these things. (She laughs.)

PB Let's go on. Does an individual have his own identity for all times?

S YES, UNLESS . . .

LH And this seems to have to do with free will.

S THE ENTITY HAS THE SAME IDENTITY ALL THROUGH A SERIES OF INCARNATIONS UNLESS HE IS THE ONE WHO HAS FAILED TO KEEP ANY PART OF HIS BARGAIN, AND THROUGH HIS OWN FREE WILL HAS ALLOWED HIMSELF TO DETERIORATE BEYOND THE LEVEL OF BEING ABLE TO BE MOTIVATED BY OUTSIDE FORCES. IN THIS CASE THE ENTITY OR SOUL-BEING OR ENERGY PART OF THAT ONE GOES INTO A POOL THROUGH WHICH OTHER BEINGS MAY BE FORMED IN TIME. HOWEVER, THIS IS NOT TO SAY THAT NEW SOULS ARE FORMED, BUT JUST RE-MERGING OF SOME OF THE LESSER QUANTITIES OR QUALITIES.

PB Do individuals merge at the other end as they reach higher levels?

LH Then, rather than feeling like a merging, I seem to come out like this. (She makes a picture like a fountain.) And this goes back to that question you asked about self-governing. It feels like, as I reach up here, they are not self-governing, but the All governs the All. In that same sense, all beings seem to merge again, but not on an individual basis.

PB Is the individual progress of an entity similar to our earth progress? For example, when we graduate from grammar school, we start junior high school, then high school, college, so that we are learning each stage of life as a beginner?

S THIS IS WHY IT IS MOST DIFFICULT TO DESCRIBE TO THOSE WHO ARE STILL UPON THE EARTH THE ULTIMATE GOAL THAT THEY ARE SEACHING FOR, FOR THOSE AREAS OF LIFE ARE AS DIFFICULT FOR MAN TO EVEN TRY TO COMPREHEND AS IT IS FOR A CHILD WHO BEGINS KINDERGARTEN TO TAKE ON THE RESPONSIBILITIES OF EARNING A LIVING AND SUPPORTING A FAMILY. THE TWO WORLDS, OR STAGES OF CONSCIOUSNESS, ARE THAT FAR APART. ONLY MORE SO.

PB But, as an entity reaches a certain level, a new door is opened to him and he steps through as a beginner again?

S YES, BUT EACH TIME HE CARRIES WITH HIM THE KNOWLEDGE THAT HE HAS THUS FAR EARNED.

PB What happens to a Mozart after the final life of accomplishment?

S FROM THE POINT OF VIEW OF MANKIND, AT THIS TIME, THERE IS NO FINAL LIFE, FOR THERE IS A CONSTANT EVOLVING. IT IS BEYOND THE POINT, VIEWING FROM THE HUMAN STANDPOINT. IT IS THE BECOMING LIGHT, ENERGY, DIFFUSION IN ITSELF.

LH And these seem to be: LIGHT, hyphen, hyphen, ENERGY, hyphen, hyphen, DIFFUSION. Not combined.

PB I was thinking of a Mozart as an overly-specialized entity, not well-rounded or balanced.

S THIS ONE WILL RETURN UNTIL THERE IS A ROUNDING OUT OF THOSE QUALITITES THAT ARE NECESSARY. IT IS ONLY THAT THIS PARTICULAR SOUL MUST BE EXTREMELY CAREFUL THAT HE DOES NOT WITHDRAW WITHIN AND BECOME CLOSED TO OUTSIDE INTERESTS OR GROWTH. THESE WILL COME IN OTHER LIFETIMES EVEN THOUGH HE NEEDS TO LEARN THEM MANY TIMES IN A VERY DIFFICULT MANNER. THE EXTREME PUSHING-OUT OF ONE AREA ONLY HAS TO BE COMPENSATED FOR AT ANOTHER TIME.

PB Can an entity, while advancing, fall further behind?

LH It says "NO."

(That was encouraging.)

PB Is an entity a unit of energy force?

LH It seems to be more of a transmitting station. It is a station which receives and sends off. It is not energy itself, but is a reflection of energy.

PB Describe an energy force.

S IT IS A CENTRAL POINT FROM WHICH RADIATIONS GO OUT. IT IS NOT NECESSARILY THE BEGINNING OF THOSE RADIATIONS, BUT A TRANSMITTER OR CONDUCTOR OF THEM. ALL THINGS THAT ARE ARE ENERGY RADIATION. AND ALL THINGS AID, ABET, ADD TO OR SUBTRACT FROM OTHER AREAS OF BEING SO THAT ALL ENERGY IS BEING INTERCHANGEABLY MIXED.

LH I don't know. I feel like I'm wandering because all I'm seeing are a lot of little black dots running. And some attract one way and some another, and some give off, and some add or draw from.

(The pictures shown to her were often amusing while instructive.)

PB Is there a set number of entities?

S THERE IS A SET NUMBER OF ENERGY FORCES ON THE EARTH PLANE, AND THOSE WHICH HAVE BEEN ASSIGNED TO THAT

PLANE. HOWEVER, THERE IS NOT A SET NUMBER OF ENTITIES
AS SUCH.

PB   Do individual entities move in groups so that they are
continuously being reincarnated together?

S   AS A RULE, FOR THESE ARE THE ONES WHO ARE ABLE TO
WORK WELL TOGETHER. THEY HAVE BEEN ABLE TO BLEND
THEIR FORCES. HOWEVER, THERE ARE SOME AREAS IN WHICH
ONE WILL FIND THAT HE IS RISING TO A HIGHER LEVEL AND
THUS WILL MERGE WITH A NEW SOUL GROUP IN A SERIES OF
INCARNATIONS UNTIL HE HAS WORKED OUT ANY OF HIS OWN
PROBLEMS OR PROBLEMS WITH OTHERS IN THIS PARTICULAR
GROUP. THIS, AGAIN, IS A PROCESS OF PROGRESSION.

PB   Could Universal Mind be like the ocean with each entity
as a drop of water?

S   AMEN.

PB   And then it's individual until it returns to the ocean?

S   YES, AND IT IS ALSO INDIVIDUAL IN THAT EACH ONE WILL
ALWAYS MANIFEST, TO A CERTAIN DEGREE, THE QUALITITES
THAT MAKE HIM A FACET OF THAT ALL. HOWEVER, THIS IS
ALSO THE WAY IN WHICH ALL CAN REACH THE MINDS OF
OTHERS, AND THIS IS WHERE THERE IS A BLENDING INTO THE
UNIVERSAL FORCE OR MIND.

PB   Define Mind.

S   MIND, AS THE OVERALL MIND, IS THAT WHICH IS THE IN-
STIGATOR AND MOTIVATOR BEHIND ALL THE SMALL SEG-
MENTS OF MIND KNOWN AS MAN. MIND IS THE PACESETTER.
MIND IS THAT WHICH CONVERTS ALL ENERGY INTO MASS.
MIND IS THE PART WHICH IS ALSO ETERNAL AND THE STRUC-
TURE WITHIN WHICH ALL THINGS ARE FORMED.

(What a beautiful definition. They were always impressive.)

LH Mind must be disciplined. It feels like a powerhouse, and if it's disciplined, it's charged; and if it's undisciplined it's destruction. That's capital M—Mind.

PB Do entities draw on group experiences as well as individual experience in their growth patterns?

S Yes.

PB Are these groups of various sizes, for example, like a tribe, then a town, a city, a state, a country, and eventually the world, and then groups of worlds or even universes?

S Yes, to some degree, and yet there are . . .

LH It seems like there are soul groups that may have part of the group in Africa and part in America and part around the world. They seem together on a different plane, as though they work in communication with each other even though they are not closely related geographically. It looks like this: (She draws a dot for the world with circles around it.) This is the world and there seems to be layer after layer. The soul groups seem to be in layers as much as in particular type groups.

PB Would this be in line with Galbraith's description of the modern corporate structure with the circles within circles, rather than the family-tree type of structure?

(Peter had just finished reading Galbraith's book.)

S Yes.

PB How soon does an entity reincarnate?

S This is not a set pattern or rule. It is dependent on the free will of that particular entity. Also upon the needs of that entity. If it is one that has been greatly damaged or hurt in one particular incarnation, and is not pliable or workable in the between-stage, it is then incarnated rather quickly and

CAUSED TO HAVE A SHORT LIFE SO THAT IT WILL COME IN AS A MORE PLIABLE FORM. IT MAY THEN CHOOSE ITS TIME AND PLACE TO RELEARN THE LESSON IT MISSED. OR IT MAY GO ON TO NEW LESSONS IF IT PERHAPS CHOSE SOME THAT WERE TOO DIFFICULT.

PB   Are there other entities at higher levels that are learning from man's experiences?

S   THERE ARE THOSE WHO OVERSEE. THERE ARE ALSO THOSE . . .

LH   And I don't know what to call those inbetween . . . like life between another life . . . anyway, there seems to be a lot of learning process that goes on in the between cycle . . .

S   . . . THAT IS GIVEN TO MAN TO WITNESS AND TO GROW THROUGH THE EXPERIENCE OF THOSE OTHERS IF HE WILL SO CHOOSE. HOWEVER, THERE ARE THOSE WHO WILL ONLY LEARN BY BURNING THEIR OWN FINGERS.

PB   Is the in-between a definite plane, or is this a sort of suspense situation?

LH   It feels like a plane, because I walk.

(Once again a picture experience helps the explanation.)

PB   What would be an average number of physical reincarnations before an entity might reach a wholly spiritual plane?

LH   This sounds ridiculous, but it seems to be up around 900.

PB   Do we go through various levels of spiritual and soul reincarnations in the same sense that we experience physical reincarnations?

LH   The soul seems to stay whole . . . like it travels right along parallel with bodies as they go in and out. The body seems changing, but the soul doesn't. Soul, as I seem to be getting it, is a clearheaded thing that moves along and sees all. Spirit, when it comes down, seems to get clouded with each incarnation. But soul seems unclouded or straight-travelling.

PB Thank you. As interesting as this is, our time is up and we'll have to stop.

Now we all found ourselves looking forward to the spiritual lift we felt in the presence of these inspiring answers. For each of our weekly schedules this was an hour of inner excitement.

As we gathered together there was no time lost in getting on with our communication.

PB How many planes or levels of existence are there?

LH I seem to be getting the number 9, and it seems to be in relation to this world, or while it's still attached to or revolving around this particular world.

PB Could this be the world as we think of it, or is it a universe?

LH No, it seems to be this world, and each time the string gets looser, like by the time they've reached this ninth plane, they're ready to move on to something else.

PB Some people believe that as man is harmonious, earth stays together, and as man fights, it may fall apart. Is the earth, in fact, held in man's consciousness?

LH Again I get the word AMEN.

PB I was going to ask if it is manifested by other consciousnesses for man.

S   IT WAS BEGUN ON THE OTHER LEVEL. HOWEVER, MAN IS NOW
    RESPONSIBLE FOR HIS OWN HOLDING TOGETHER OF THIS
    AREA. IT IS NECESSARY THAT HE SEE THE FAR-REACHING EF-
    FECTS OF HIS MIND, HIS THINKING, HIS ABILITY TO CREATE.
    IT IS NECESSARY THAT MAN TAKE ON THIS RESPONSIBILITY
    FOR HIMSELF. IT CAN BE DONE FOR HIM, BUT THIS IS NO
    LONGER NECESSARY.

PB Is space, as we think of it, occupied by many beings in
    one spot at different times?

S   IT IS FAR MORE CROWDED THAN YOU WOULD BELIEVE. YES, IT
    IS TRUE THAT MANY DIFFERENT FORMS OF LIFE CAN OCCUPY
    THE SAME SPACE AS YOU RECOGNIZE IT. HOWEVER, IT IS NOT
    ESSENTIAL. THE MAJORITY OF THOSE WHO OCCUPY THE SAME
    SPACE AS YOU DO ARE THOSE WHO ARE LEARNING THROUGH
    YOUR EXPERIENCE OR BY YOUR EXAMPLE. THIS IS NOT A
    BLANKET SITUATION, BUT ON THE MOST PART.

PB At what levels does the male-female concept disappear?

S   THIS WILL ALWAYS APPEAR AS A VARIANCE OF THINKING
    AND A VARIANCE OF FEELINGS, FOR IN THE HIGHER REALMS
    IT IS REFERRED TO WITH THE THOUGHT THAT THE FEMALE IS
    THE MORE TENDER, THE MORE SYMPATHETIC, THE MORE RE-
    LIANT. AND THE MALE IS THE MORE PROGRESSIVE, AGGRES-
    SIVE, STRENGTH-GIVING MEMBER. BUT THESE TWO MUST
    FIND A BALANCE, FOR ONLY BY STRESSING ONE CAN THE
    OTHER BE SEEN.

(So we shall always be these lovely counterparts.)

LH And then they go up like an arrow point. They seem to
    merge, but still the terms seem to be there.

PB We have been talking about various planes that are real-
    ly more like circles. Are these circles also symbolic of
    spheres?

LH Yes, and it says "SPHERES OF GROWTH AND SPHERES OF IN-
    FLUENCE." And they seem to be different.

PB Now, we understand that both a circle and a sphere are considered to be infinite. We also believe that there are different-sized infinities. Is this correct?

S WELL, THE CIRCLE IS INFINITE, TRUE, AND YET IT HAS ITS BOUNDARIES. THIS IS WHAT IS IMPLIED IN THE FACT THAT THE INFINITE IS ONLY SO FAR AS CAN BE COMPREHENDED.

PB Then, could there be several small infinities within a large infinity?

S YES, AND THERE ARE OTHER NAMES TO THESE AREAS, BUT THEY ARE NOT UNDERSTANDABLE AT THIS POINT. CONTINUE TO GROW WITH THIS AND SEEK WITHIN YOURSELF.

PB And could these various infinities, like transparent or etherial spheres, overlap?

S YES, FOR VARYING PURPOSES. THERE ARE THOSE AREAS WHICH OVERLAP FOR POWER, AND THERE ARE THOSE WHICH OVERLAP FOR A TRANSFERENCE OF GROWTH.

LH And that doesn't feel complete, but I don't get any more.

(Apparently it bothered her that she wasn't getting a complete answer, so she started making circles again with her pen and staring ahead as she listened to the next question.)

PB Could an entity best be thought of as a growing sphere?

S YES.

LH And when you say that, it feels like a million little lights, and around each light there's a little sphere of light. And some of them are together and some are not.

PB Now, would groups of entities be like overlapping, interwined, and possibly interlocking spheres?

S YES.

PB   Is it correct that these interlocking, overlapping groups of spheres need not be geographically near each other nor necessarily in the same earth or star time?

S   AMEN.

PB   O.K., are these spheres at various vibration levels?

S   THIS IS THE TOTAL ANSWER, FOR AS THEY REACH A DEGREE OF VIBRATION, THEY ARE THEN TRANSFERRED TO A NEW SPHERE OR A NEW LEVEL.

PB   Could spiritual advancement mean, in addition to growing as a sphere, the ability to join with other spheres, both as individual entities and as groups of entities?

S   YES. AND THIS IS THE PROGRESSION THAT TAKES PLACE ALWAYS AND EVER.

PB   How many dimensions does a sphere have?

S   HOW MANY DAYS DOES TIME HAVE?

PB   Thank you. Are there various Alls? Capital A Alls?

LH   Instead of an answer, I'm getting cones . . . like this: (She draws an elongated triangle.) It's like a baby's colored one that goes up. And this seems to be the All, rather than various Alls. They all come together in total.

PB   Yes, good. In the sense we have been discussing, are there universes beyond what we know and can conceive of, and beyond what *you* know, and those beyond you that are completely unknown as to their nature other than that they are thought to exist or be?

S   UNDER THE GUISE OF TIME AND SPACE, MANY THOUGHTS ARE GIVEN. YES, YOU HAVE BEGUN TO COMPREHEND THAT WHICH IS BEYOND, AND YET IT IS NOT CONCEIVABLE BY THE

MIND OF MAN TO IMAGINE THE LIMITLESS UNIVERSES
BEYOND ALL. . . .

LH Something . . . just a minute . . .

S THE ONENESS THAT IS ACHIEVED IN ETERNITY IS MORE THAN
CAN BE GIVEN TO THE FINITE MIND. THE ALL THAT YOU
SPOKE OF IS MORE THAN EVEN YOU CAN IMAGINE. EACH
EARTH IS AS A CELL WITHIN A GIANT BODY. AND SO, BY
THIS, YOU MAY HAVE A SLIGHT COMPARISON TO THE SIZE OF
THE ALL.

PB Is there more beyond what *you* can conceive?

S I AM THOUGHT AND TIME AND ENERGY. I AM LIMITLESS AND
EXPANDABLE. I AM AWARE OF THE LIMITLESS BOUNDARIES,
AND YET EVEN I HAVE NOT BEEN THERE.

PB Am I, in my true form, limitless and expandable?

S YOU ARE A PART OF THAT. YOU CAN NEVER BE THE ALL, BUT
YOU MUST ALWAYS BE A SECTION, AN INFINITY WITHIN THE
INFINITY.

PB Is there a constructive purpose in my communicating
with Universal Intelligence through Mrs. Huett at this
time?

S IT'S HELPFUL TO THE END THAT WHEN AN IDEA NEEDS TO BE
SEEDED, IT CAN BE GIVEN TO THOSE WHO WILL ACT UPON IT
OR USE IT IN A HELPFUL MANNER TO MANKIND.

PB In our human form, we seem to be three-dimensional
beings. Do we learn to become four-dimensional beings
as we grow, or are we, in fact, four-dimensional beings
playing games by putting on blinders?

LH When you said "three-dimensional," I was getting
"five." Now, I don't know what the fifth would be.

S   THERE IS THE REALM OF FIVE DIMENSIONS WITHIN MAN AND
    SOME OF THOSE WHO WALK THE EARTH ARE WELL AWARE OF
    THESE REALMS.

LH Like one out of every million, whatever that may be.

S   THE SOUL IS NOT TOTALLY AWARE OF THIS WHILE WALKING
    THE EARTH PLANE, BUT THOSE WHO ARE HIGHLY EVOLVED
    KNOW WITHIN THEM THAT THEY HAVE THIS POTENTIAL. THE
    BLINDER. . . .

LH It feels more like a curtain which drops at birth, but
    some people have the ability to lift that curtain and peek
    through.

PB My next question was to be about the fifth dimension,
    although I have never read nor seen anything about it.

LH I've never heard of it before. There seem to be five
    within this . . . I'll use the term "universe," but I don't
    know what to call it. But when we progress beyond
    that, I feel seven and eventually nine. I couldn't con-
    ceive of what they might be.

PB If all is mental, could the fifth dimension be a concept of
    materializing and dematerializing?

S   THIS IS ONE OF THE AREAS IN WHICH THOSE OF THE HIGH
    FOURTH DIMENSION ARE ABLE TO EXPERIMENT. IT IS THE
    BEGINNING. ACTUALLY, WHEN ONE IS IN THE FIFTH DIMEN-
    SION, THIS COMES AND MOVES RATHER EASILY. IT IS A PART
    OF THEIR NATURE.

LH I seem to get the ability to travel at will, and I can't tell
    whether the body follows or not. But I feel very free in
    the fifth dimension.

PB Is there a physical manifestation in fifth dimension?

LH It says "YES."

PB Could I learn to travel by dematerializing in this life?

LH I can't get you to dematerialize, but I can get your whole body to lift up. This doesn't seem to be like astral travel. It is more like. . . levitation of your thoughts, not of articles.

PB Have I done this in the past?

LH You seem to have witnessed it.

PB Is the development of a third eye a new dimension?

S No, THIS WAS A SOURCE OF POWER AND ENLIGHTENMENT THAT WAS GIVEN TO MAN WHEN HE FIRST CAME UPON THE EARTH. HOWEVER, IT HAS BEEN A SUBJECT THAT HAS BEEN DIMLY PLACED ASIDE. IT IS A NEW DIMENSION FOR EACH SOUL, EACH BEING, THAT ENCOUNTERS IT. BUT IT IS NOT A NEW GROWTH.

PB Thank you again. This seems to be our longest session ever, and I fear Mrs. Huett may have run out of time. We'll carry on another day with more questions I have for you.

(Lenora gave a deep sigh, dropping her arms down to her sides wearily, but with a great sense of satisfaction. We were all very excited about the outpouring we'd just heard.)

The next time we met the questioning began with the subject of our own particular futures in this lifetime.

PB I have a few questions of a personal nature for your Source.
   What moves do you see ahead for us?

(Some friends had invited us to take a trip to Canada with them where Peter became very enthused about Vancouver Island.)

LH I see you make three major moves before you die: straight north, then east, then southward, perhaps to Colorado, but I can't exactly name the state.

PB What is the purpose?

LH To be mobile in order to benefit each of you and mankind.

PB What work do you see ahead for me?

LH I see you work with new things, and when it's almost finished, you move on. You're not flighty. You have good potential. You are recognized by your work. It is not necessary to be top man in any field. Continue as you are going. It is necessary for your fulfillment. When you feel you have grasped the situation, move on.

PB Why do I feel such a restlessness?

LH You have a lust for life, a desire to taste the good things. You are not left behind. You are like a boy at a banquet who hasn't had time to get to all of it.

PB Why are Jane and I together?

LH You and your wife have good balance. You liberate each other with your different natures—yours fast, hers slow. The combination causes much to be accomplished. You would drive yourself crazy with someone of your own nature.

PB We are considering making a major move away from the city to a simpler life style. Can your Source tell us where we are to settle?

LH I don't get names very well, but I'll ask.
(There was a long silence)
    No. Sorry. Nothing comes.

PB Perhaps you could tell us what parallel on the map.

LH That doesn't seem to come either, but I see a picture of a white whale.

(We both laughed at the ridiculous image.)

PB Thank you. And now on to our general questions: Why are there so many entities that seem to be concerned with saving mankind?

S IT IS A MATTER OF SPIRITUAL PRIDE WITH THESE ENTITIES. IT IS A MATTER THAT THEY FEEL THIS CAN BE DONE AND THEY ARE DETERMINED TO HELP BRING IT ABOUT. THEY KNOW THAT THROUGH THE SAVING OF THIS, IT WILL ALSO ADD TO THE POWER AND BENEFIT THAT THEY ARE ABLE TO RECEIVE IN THEIR OWN REALM. THIS IS ABLE TO BOOST THEM TO EVEN HIGHER REALMS, FOR EACH SOUL IS A MATTER OF POWER.

LH And it feels like wattage power.

S THEY ARE ALSO ABLE TO SEE THE NON-NECESSITY OF THE WASTE THAT GOES ON. AND THROUGH THIS THEY ARE DETERMINED TO HELP CHANGE THE TIDE OF TIME. THEY KNOW THAT AS MANKIND IS SAVED FROM A DESTRUCTION CAUSED BY HIMSELF, HE WILL THEN BE OF A HIGHER VIBRATION SO THAT HE, IN TURN, MAY BE ABLE TO HELP THE LOWER FORCES OR LOWER FORMS OF LIFE. THIS WILL, IN ESSENCE, ADD TO THEIR BAND.

PB Speaking of bands, where are the bulk of the Atlanteans?

LH It feels reincarnated at this point, and by that, it feels like 75%.

PB What other types of entities are there such as the Atlanteans?

S LEMURIANS AND MU. IN THE MEDICAL FIELD THERE ARE MANY LEMURIANS AT PRESENT.

LH Atlanteans feel like the scientific fields: science of the elements or space science. This last feels like pyramids, moving giant objects, leverage.

PB What percentage are they presently?

LH It feels like 30%. This feels just traces.

PB Are my wife and I in the same group?

S   YOU HAVE COME MANY TIMES TOGETHER. YOU ARE OF THE SAME SOUL SECT AND ARE IN COMPATIBLE VIBRATION WITH EACH OTHER. YES, YOU ARE OF THE SAME INCARNATIONS.

LH And that seems to leap-frog back, like if not at the same time, you go back in the same straight line.

PB Are we related to the Atlanteans?

S   YES.

LH But when you were an Atlantean, it feels like you looked down your nose at them, because I feel disapproval of something. It's as though you watched scientists at work at that time and you would say, "Why are they so slow? Why don't they see what they are doing?" It's as though your mind was ahead of what they were doing, and yet you didn't involve yourself with it or try to step in and help them. It's like you just stood there and said, "If they could see clearly, they would do it otherwise."

PB What else do you see in my past lives?

LH In the year 300 A.D. I see you in Turkey with a long dagger. You were a street fighter, angry at the world. In the year 1300 you are spiritually at peace. I see you in Tibet as a businessman. Your whole family was wiped out in an accident. It looks like drowning.

Then I see you in Iran in a long robe, a traveller with wares, a gatherer of information, carrying it from place to place. There is death by a long dagger. You are way-laid, an accident.

In a Lhasa monastery you are controlled and disciplined. Other monks feel you could learn humility, but you don't need it.

You and your wife have been helpmates before. You both chose this again.

PB What about Jane's past lives?

LH I see beautiful shimmering gold fabrics. It's a feeling of a harem. She was a gift, the wife of one who had many wives, but she felt no resentment. I see her in colorful pantaloons in Persia. She was contented, free to be what she wanted to be. I see her feeling free and yet part of a household with a master. She has loved beauty and fine things. She has never misused wealth. In many lifetimes she has been connected with the arts and the finer things of life. No nursing or teaching. Her spiritual side is in the arts rather than as a nun. Three times she has had mystical lives. I don't see her doing anything menial. It's all etherial and light and artistic.

(They say you feel a visceral impact when a former life seems true. I had that strongly about the harem picture and could even picture Peter in what was described about him. I was part of that family that drowned.)

PB Thank you. What do you see in future lives for us?

LH For you a worldwide brotherhood. Ecumenical. No connection with money or politics. Something like teaching people. Lots of travel with a group of men. Close-knit. Helping others learn. And for your wife in a future life I see no marriage. She is teaching women. I see her in the center of a group based in the U.S.—south central—a desert retreat. I see your heads as radios—you and Jane—in strong mental contact.

(When we were driving home Peter told me about his own cold feel of the dagger when he was travelling on foot with wares and messages he sold.)

We gathered together a few days later:

PB   What is the contract we enter into when we are born on earth?

S   THE CONTRACT THAT ONE ENTERS INTO AS HE ENTERS THIS LIFE EXPERIENCE IS ONE IN WHICH HE ALONE OR WITH HELPERS CAN VIEW HIS PAST LIVES AND INCARNATIONS, HIS PAST EXPERIENCES, HIS PAST LEARNING, AND HIS REACTIONS TO THESE. AND THROUGH THIS EVALUATION, CAN DETERMINE THOSE THINGS WHICH ARE STILL NECESSARY TO COME INTO HIS PATH SO THAT HE CAN COME CLOSER TO BEING THE COMPLETE OR ROUNDED SOUL THAT IS NECESSARY FOR HIM. IT IS THEN THAT HE DETERMINES HIS BIRTH SIGN, HIS BIRTH TIME, HIS BIRTH AREA, SO THAT BY FINDING THE PROPER FAMILY, THE PROPER SOULS TO INCARNATE WITH, THE PROPER TIMING FOR HIS TOOLS, HE WILL THEN BE ABLE TO CHALLENGE THOSE AREAS THAT NEED THE WORK.

PB   Are there contracts and agreements entered into at various levels?

S   YES, AND MANY TIMES BY SIGNING THE ONE CONTRACT THERE ARE VARIOUS AREAS THAT CAN BE WORKED ON, BOTH FROM THE SPIRITUAL, MENTAL AND PHYSICAL ASPECTS. MANY TIMES THE PHYSICAL BODY IS A VERY IMPORTANT PART OF THIS. THUS THE NEED FOR SOME TO COME IN A CRIPPLED FORM. AND YET THIS CAN ALSO GIVE THEM THE THRUST FORWARD OF AN EXTREMELY STRONG BODY IN A FUTURE LIFE.

PB   Explain the term, "offer made, the chance is given."

S THE SOUL HAS THE OVERVIEW OF THE LIFE THAT IS TO COME. THERE ARE MANY FINE POINTS WHICH ARE NOT ALWAYS SEEN CLEARLY, AND THIS IS NOT NECESSARY. IT IS THE OVERALL VIEW THAT IS EXTREMELY IMPORTANT TO THE TOTAL GROWTH. THE CHANCE IS GIVEN TO CHALLENGE THIS AS ONE WILL. IT IS NOT NECESSARY THAT IT ALWAYS BE ACCEPTED. MANY TIMES YOU CAN BYPASS A LESSON AS IT SEEMINGLY COMES TOWARD YOU IF YOU FEEL THAT YOU WILL DO BADLY OR FAIL TO PASS THE TEST, SO TO SPEAK. THE OFFER OF AN EXCESS LESSON OR EXTRACURRICULAR WORK IS NOT ONE THAT WOULD BE A DENIAL OF SELF IF YOU BYPASS IT.

PB Does an entity have to pay its Karmic debt in the next life, or are there skips that leapfrog over incarnations?

S THERE CAN BE MANY SKIPS, MANY PERIODS OF TIME, DEPENDING ON THE SOUL'S EVOLVEMENT AND THE ABILITIES AND STRENGTHS THAT HAVE BEEN GAINED. IF A PROBLEM IS TOO BIG TO BEAR IN ONE LIFE . . . AND THERE MAY BE A DEEP SOUL SCAR THAT FOLLOWS THROUGH WITH ONE . . . THEY WOULD NOT NECESSARILY BE ABLE TO HANDLE THAT IN THE FOLLOWING LIFE. MUCH IS DETERMINED IN THE BETWEEN-LIFE PERIODS IN WHICH A SOUL OR HIS HELPERS CAN MORE THOROUGHLY EVALUATE HIS PROGRESS AND HIS ABILITIES.

PB Are some entities sacrificed so other entities may fulfill their learning needs?

LH It says: ONLY BY CHOICE.

S THOSE WHO ARE SACRIFICED HAVE BEEN GIVEN THE FOREWARNING BEFORE THEY ENTER THE LIFE EXPERIENCE THAT IT WILL BE NECESSARY FOR THEM TO LAY DOWN THEIR LIVES. HOWEVER, THIS IS VERY BENEFICIAL TO THEM IN THEIR OWN KARMA, FOR THEY CAN THEN PROVE THEIR WORTH AND THEIR LACK OF FEAR. THEY CAN PROVE THEIR OWN TRUE METTLE.

PB Do those sacrificing accumulate Karmic points?

S   TRUE. YOU HAVE SAID IT.

PB   What is Karma?

S   KARMA IS LAW. KARMA IS JUST. KARMA IS REACTION. KAR-
     MA IS THAT WHICH IS SET INTO EFFECT BY EACH PLANT, ANI-
     MAL, ATOM, BEING, GROUP, FORCE . . .

LH   It seems to grow with each thing.

S   . . . NATION, WORLD, UNIVERSE. KARMA IS THE LAW OF
     ALL THINGS. IT IS THE GOODNESS AND THE BADNESS THAT AP-
     PEARS TO BE MADE MANIFEST. IT IS NEITHER. IT IS ACTION
     AND REACTION. IT IS LAW.

PB   Wonderful. Describe the various tasks that are set for a
     soul to accomplish in a lifetime.

S   A TASK OF ACCEPTANCE. ACCEPTANCE CAN COVER MANY
     AREAS. BOTH ACCEPTANCE OF SELF, ACCEPTING THOSE
     DUTIES WHICH ABOUND AROUND YOU, ACCEPTING OTHER
     SOULS AT THEIR OWN LEVEL OF GROWTH OR AT THEIR OWN
     TIMING. ACCEPTING THE LESSONS OF WEALTH AND OF
     POVERTY. ACCEPTING LIMITATION AS IT IS NECESSARY, AND
     YET NOT ACCEPTING THAT WHICH IS NOT NECESSARY. THE
     LESSON OF LOVE. TO SEE IF ONE IS ABLE TO LOVE ALL SOULS
     EQUALLY. TO LOVE ALL AREAS OF LIFE, SUCH AS THE ROCKS,
     THE PLANTS, THE AIR, THE GOOD AND THE BAD.
         ALL OF THESE AREAS MUST BE JUDGED AND EVALUATED.
     MANY TIMES A PERSON CAN FIND THAT HE CAN LOVE HIS
     FELLOW HUMAN WITH AN ALL-CONSUMING LOVE, AND YET
     HATE THE ANIMALS THAT ARE UPON THE EARTH. THIS IS NOT
     A TRUE LOVE AND THIS MUST BE WORKED WITH. HE WILL
     THEN BE GIVEN THE CHANCE TO BECOME, POSSIBLY, A ZOO
     KEEPER OR ONE WHO WORKS WITH ANIMALS. HE MAY BE
     THROWN INTO THE LION'S DEN. THERE ARE MANY WAYS IN
     WHICH ONE CAN BE TESTED AND PROVEN IN OTHER AREAS OF
     LIFE.

THE LESSONS OF SELF-WORTH, SELF-EVALUATION, HONESTY, PRETENSE, ETC. ARE ALL PART OF THE TOTAL CHARACTER. THE FACETS ARE AS MANY AS THE GRAINS OF SAND UPON THE EARTH. THEY ARE NOT DEFINED AS BLACK AND WHITE. THEY ARE VARYING SHADES AND DEGREES. ONE SOUL MAY FIND THAT IT CANNOT COMPLETELY LOVE ITS ENVIRONMENT BECAUSE IT NEVER FEELS THAT IT IS AT HOME UPON THE EARTH PLANE. THIS WILL MEAN THAT SOUL MUST CONTINUE TO INCARNATE INDEFINITELY UNTIL HE CAN LOVE THE EARTH ENVIRONMENT. SOME OF THESE LACKS DO CONTINUE ON WITH THAT SOUL INTO ANOTHER REALM.

PB Define love.

S   LOVE IS ONE OF THE MOST DIFFICULT. . . .

LH It's a boxed word.

S   . . . DIFFICULT TO DEFINE BECAUSE IT IS A FEELING RATHER THAN A CONSCIOUS EFFORT. LOVE IS SOMETHING THAT ALL PEOPLE MUST EXPERIENCE. IT IS THE FEELING OF ONENESS WITH ALL. IT IS A SYRUPY HONEY FEELING. IT IS A LACK OF JUDGMENT . . .

LH Not judgment. Wait.

S   . . . LACK OF JUDGMENTAL CHARACTER. IT IS A LACK OF DEFINING. IT IS A LACK OF SET RULES. IT IS A FLOWINGNESS, A TOTAL UNDERSTANDING, A COMPREHENSION, AN EMPATHY.

PB Does it relate to hate?

S   HATE AND LOVE ARE VERY SIMILAR, BUT HATE IS THE DEFINING OF THE THINGS THAT LOVE CANNOT DEFINE.

LH Because as soon as you say "hate" I take the same words I had for love and I put a box around them. This doesn't seem to mean limited, but it's like bringing them into . . . for instance, where love was not judgmental, hate is judgmental. But it's the same word—boxed in.

PB That was excellent. I think we've covered enough material today and thank you very much.

LH Did you get what you wanted?

PB Fascinating material. You were certainly clear.

LH No one ever asked those questions through me. Sometime I'd like to hear that tape.

PB You will.

(He made an appointment for the following week and as we left her telephone was ringing. We wanted to hear the tape again ourselves. That night we played back some of the beginning tapes. On a second hearing some of the information seemed entirely new to me, and some struck me with new light, new meanings. It was very exciting.)

With plans for another trip to Vancouver Island, along with our business responsibilities, our lives became too busy for me to keep typing the material from the tapes. At the next meeting with Lenora, Peter continued his questions on reincarnation.

PB How does a child genius such as Mozart come to be and why?

LH This says YOU ALREADY KNOW.

S   YOU KNOW THE VALUE OF REINCARNATION. YOU KNOW THE VALUE OF LIVES CARRIED OVER. YOU KNOW THE ABILITY OF MANY WHO HAVE DEVELOPED HIGHLY IN ONE LIFE. MOZART WAS ONE THAT HAD DEVELOPED HIGHLY THROUGH SEVERAL LIFETIMES.

LH It feels like five or six had pulled together into the one. Not five or six entities but five or six lives that culminated in that.

S   THE ABILITIES ARE THEN MANIFEST, FOR A CHILD IS LESS PRONE TO BLOCK OUT THE PAST MEMORIES THAN AN ADULT IS. THOSE THINGS WHICH COME FORTH IN CHILDHOOD ARE VERY VALUABLE, FOR THAT IS WHEN THEY CAN BEST EXPRESS THEIR GREATEST TALENTS. WATCH CHILDREN CAREFULLY.

PB Man has free will. Does soul have free will?

S   THE SOUL HAS PURPOSE.

PB Describe in detail the level or realm where the soul resides.

S   THE SOUL IS. AND THAT'S A CAPITAL I. IT IS NOT AT A PARTICULAR PLACE AT A PARTICULAR TIME. IT IS NOT AN ENTITY AS YOUR ARE ABLE TO VISUALIZE MANKIND. IT IS NOT A FREE-FLOATING THING SUCH AS YOU ARE ABLE TO VISUALIZE SPIRIT. THE SOUL IS.

LH And it repeats that.

S   THE SOUL IS A PART OF THE ALL, THE TOTAL, JUST AS GOD IS. HOWEVER, A SOUL CAN BE IMCOMPLETE. THE PURPOSE OF THE SOUL IS TO FIND ITS COMPLETENESS, ITS WHOLENESS, AND TO RETURN TO THE ALL.

LH The soul seems to feel like. . . when you look at a comic strip and see this little cloud above people when they're talking. The soul seems to be like that. Like it's aware. And that's all. There doesn't seem to be form, shape, plane, time, anything.

PB The soul is aware. Is it aware at the astral level?

LH No. It feels above that. Well, it is aware, but it's higher than that.

PB Is the soul aware at the astral level, the spirit level, the human level, the subconscious, unconscious and super-conscious levels?

LH Right. And it's purpose seems to be to try to make all of these aware of the other parts. . . or when they're all aware of the other parts, then the soul has something to work with and go.

PB Is the soul in spirit and body at the same time?

S   THE SOUL IS EVER NEAR OR AWARE OF THE BODY. IT IS A PART OF THE SPIRIT.

PB Does the soul exist on other planets at the same time as here with man?

S   NOT EXIST, BUT IS AWARE ON OTHER PLANETS AT THE SAME TIME. YES.

PB In other words, each individual entity's individual soul is aware of other planets at the same time?

LH Yes, but it doesn't seem to have other bodies on other planets. It feels like it's aware of what is going on, because it seems to be in communication with all things, like it can tap in at any point, because I'm seeing a tremendous switchboard.

PB Has an entity had lives on each of the other planets?

S   TRUE.

PB And the soul is aware of these?

S   TRUE.

PB So that the position or relationship of these planets to the individual entity then causes a certain relationship or balance?

S   YES. THESE DIFFERENT PLANET LIVES HAVE BEEN ABLE TO PROVIDE MANY OF THE STRONG POINTS AND STRONG CHAR-

ACTERISTICS THAT NOW ABIDE UPON THE EARTH. VERY LIT-
TLE OF THE NEGATIVE IS BROUGHT OVER, FOR THEY ARE
NOT. . .

LH Anything that's negative, they've worked through before they were able to leave that area.

PB As they are doing here?

S YES.

PB Does the human spirit of each of our earth lives continue to exist in Spirit?

LH Yes, but it feels like layer upon layer upon layer. In other words, like my past lives seem to be very close around me. So it doesn't feel like free-floating spirits of past me. I don't know. I have no idea what any of the great religions may say. I hadn't even thought of this.

PB Are human fears in life detrimental to soul development?

S NO, BUT THEY ARE A PART OF THE SOUL DEVELOPMENT. THEY ARE A PART THAT IS NECESSARY TO LEARN TO ELIMINATE, FOR ALL FACETS OF FEAR ARE LACK OF ENERGY OR LACK OF OUT-GOINGNESS. AND THIS IS NECESSARY TO BE ERASED BEFORE THE SOUL CAN AGAIN BE COMPLETE. IF IT IS NOT ERASED IN ONE LIFE, THERE ARE SEVERAL WAYS IN WHICH IT CAN BE HELPED WITH OTHERS.

PB Is pain for soul growth?

S NOT BODILY PAIN, FOR MANY TIMES THIS IS SELF-INFLICTED. HOWEVER, PAIN IS A VERY GOOD MONITOR OF HOW A PERSON IS ABLE TO ACCEPT THESE OTHER AREAS OF LIFE. IF ONE IS CONSTANTLY LOOKING FOR JOY AND HAPPINESS, HE WILL FIND THAT THIS IS NOT THE BEST WAY OF GROWTH. PAIN, AS BEING SELF-INFLICTED, IS NOT NECESSARY FOR GROWTH EITHER. THERE ARE MANY WHO FEEL THAT IF THEY CAN

CAUSE GREAT DAMAGE TO THEIR PHYSICAL BODY AND OVER-
COME THIS THROUGH MIND, THEY ARE THEN MAKING RAPID
GROWTH. THIS IS NOT SO.

PB   Do fear or pain help in mind or spirit growth?

S   BOTH, FOR IT TAKES THE MIND TO OVERCOME THESE, AND AS
THE MIND GROWS IN STRENGTH, SO THE SPIRIT GAINS ALSO
AND THUS ONWARD TO THE SOUL.

PB   Is the soul damaged by the whimsical, careless use of the
mind's free will?

S   NOT DAMAGED, BUT MANY TIMES RETARDED IN ITS GROWTH.

PB   Going back to the soul lives again: Now, I'm thinking of
the age of a soul. On a scale of 36 inches, a soul is old
after five inches, as you said once. Does the soul as it
gets older, get more of its growth at the spirit level between lives?

S   IT CAN. IT WILL ALSO BE MORE GAME TO TAKE ON DIFFICULT
LIVES, OR THOSE OF LESSER DEGREE, KNOWING THAT
THROUGH THESE, GREAT GROWTH CAN COME. THIS DOES NOT
NECESSARILY MEAN THAT ONE MUST PICK A PARTICULARLY
HUMBLE OR HARD-WORKING LIFE, BUT ONE WILL CHOOSE THE
MORE DIFFICULT LESSONS THAT THEY MAY BE OVERCOME. A
NEW SOUL USUALLY PICKS THE EASIER PATH, THE SOFTER
ROAD, THE SINGLE LESSON PER LIFETIME.

PB   On the 36 inch scale, what is the average spiritual development of the European souls?

LH   It feels like 8.

PB   India?

LH   Either 11 or 12.

PB   Africa?

LH   7.

PB South America?

LH There seem to be areas in South America (because I'm getting pits or holes or valleys) where it's 11, but the rest seem like 9.

PB Canada?

LH 12.

PB U.S.A.?

LH 9.

PB China?

LH Hmm, it says 4.

PB How about Russia?

LH I think it's a 10.

PB Thank you. Can the spiritual and mental parts of an entity be merged completely and become one with the soul?

S WITH THE MASTERS, YES. WITH THE AVERAGE LAYMAN, THIS IS VERY IMPROBABLE, ALTHOUGH THIS WOULD BE THE ULTIMATE GOAL THAT ALL SHOULD WORK TOWARDS. IT CAN BE DONE, BUT IT IS EXTREMELY RARE UNDER EARTH CONDITIONS.

PB Is this the final state for those entities as we know humans?

S ONLY WHEN THEY GIVE THEMSELVES OVER TO THIS PROCESS IS THIS EVEN BEGUN TO BE ACCOMPLISHED. ONLY WHEN THEY ARE TOTALLY AWARE OF THEIR MISSION ON THIS EARTH CAN THIS BE ACCOMPLISHED, AND EVEN THEN THE TOTAL COMMITMENT OR TOTAL AT-ONE-NESS IS RARE.

PB Is it easier to incarnate after the mental and spiritual parts of an entity have been made one?

S   NOT NECESSARILY, BUT IT IS A MUCH BETTER INCARNATION
    THAT IS THE RESULT OF SUCH A MERGER. IT IS THE HIGHER
    TYPES OF BEING UPON THE EARTH. IT IS THE CREATIVE SOULS.
    IT IS THOSE WHO ARE OF A WORLDLY NATURE.

LH But worldly seems really to mean ecumenical or
    worldwide, more than just worldly. And of those where
    the two are merged, this seems to take in again people
    who are here to help others: science, medicine, history,
    art, and so forth.

PB What must an entity do to bring the mental and spiritual
    parts together?

S   THE ENTITY MUST DESIRE WHOLEHEARTEDLY TO BECOME AT
    ONE WITH HIMSELF, AT ONE WITH ALL NATURE, AT ONE WITH
    HIS FELLOW MAN . . . IT IS ONLY THROUGH DOING THIS
    THAT THE MENTAL CAN OPEN A PORTION AND ALLOW THE
    SPIRITUAL TO COME IN . THE SPIRITUAL WILL PERMEATE, BUT
    WITHOUT INTRODUCTION OR INVITATION.

PB Is being manifested in human form on the earth level, in
    fact, a more beneficial state than being exclusively in
    spiritual form?

S   ONLY IN THAT IT PROMOTES GREATER UNDERSTANDING AND
    MORE FULLNESS OR ROUNDNESS TO THE SOUL, A DEEPER COM-
    PASSION, A GREATER ABILITY TO COMMUNICATE IN MORE
    WAYS THAN JUST THROUGH THOUGHT OR SOUND.

LH In the human body, a person seems to reach out at his
    own level. Spirit seems to reach down or reach those
    that are below them, instead of out to their equals.

PB What is a soul without being able to manifest or to
    incarnate?

S   THERE IS NOT, IN FACT, SUCH A THING OR ESSENCE AT THIS
    TIME. ALL HAVE BEEN OR ARE BEING MANIFEST.

PB Which is the more desirable condition: to be manifest on the human earth level, to be at the between-stage, or to be at the spirit level?

S THE SPIRIT LEVEL IN ALL ITS FORMS IS THE MOST DESIRABLE CONDITION, AND THIS IS WHAT WILL BE ULTIMATELY WITH ALL SOULS. HOWEVER, THIS IS NOT THE JUMP THAT CAN BE MADE BY MANY. THEY MUST GO THROUGH MANY TRANSITIONAL PERIODS SO THAT THEY ARE FIRST A HUMAN BEING AND WORK THROUGH THOSE PROBLEMS WHICH WOULD BIND THEM WITHIN THEMSELVES. THIS IS A PART OF THE PROCESS AND ONLY THOSE WHO CONTINUE TO INCARNATE LONG BEYOND THE NORMAL PERIOD WOULD BE CONSIDERED AS SLOW SOULS OR SLOW SPIRITS. HOWEVER, KNOW THAT THE ULTIMATE GOAL, OR THE LIGHTER AND LIGHTER THAT ONE CAN BECOME IN HIS BEING, THIS IS THE TRUE DESIRE OF ALL SOULS.

PB Thank you. Could we go back to the three or five planes of existence?

LH Well, for some reason, the lowest forms of life don't seem to be a plane. Now, maybe they are, and maybe it's a growing plane. As soon as you say "the first plane" I see an earth worm, only it's a person, come up and raise its head and begin to look around or see what's around it. And . . . ah . . . I feel very antagonistic, as though this is part of the first plane. And maybe this is also saying that this is where the emotions begin, the tie-in between emotions and mental plane, because as I raise my head or look around, I feel as though I'm very aware and realize for the first time that there are other things on the earth around me. Only I don't feel that I want to relate to them.

When I say "second plane", then it feels as though . . . almost as if I've sprouted wings, or I'm floating more, because the feeling of the body is not nearly as important. I seem to have come up to where I want to relate to people, and I feel it's a mental thing. Something where I can work with my mind and their mind, and other things are less important. The physical things still seem to be there, only they are down below us or seemingly non-essential. I feel above hand-to-hand combat or fighting. It also feels like a plane of experimentation, one in which we try many things. Trial and error.

The third plane seems to relate to love, because I get "THIRD PLANE EQUALS LOVE. THIS IS A PLANE IN WHICH MAN IS BEGINNING TO REACH FOR HIS SPIRITUAL GUIDANCE, HIS OWN AWARENESS BEING MADE MANIFEST. HE IS BEGINNING TO COMMUNICATE WITH THOSE THINGS WHICH ARE ABOVE AND BEYOND HIMSELF."

And ABOVE seems to be a symbolic word. When I say "fourth plane" I . . . I guess I'm not getting it now. Sorry.

PB It probably means you are tiring. It's been a long session, but very worthwhile.

When our adopted daughter listened to our tapes, she was curious to ask her own questions. Taking her tape recorder to Lenora's, she shared with us the communication producing these answers:

BH At what stage of development does an entity attach or become a part of the flesh being?

S   THE ENTITY, HERE BEING THE SOUL, WHICH ENTERS THE BODY, OCCURS USUALLY VERY CLOSE TO THE BIRTH TIME. IT CAN COME PRIOR TO THE BIRTH. IT CAN COME VERY SHORTLY

AFTER. OR IT CAN COME AT THE MOMENT OF BIRTH. THERE CAN EVEN BE A TWO OR THREE WEEK LEEWAY HERE.

BH When an entity agrees to enter into the cycle again, does he pre-determine how long his life will be in this cycle?

S USUALLY. THERE ARE TIMES WHEN AN ENTITY WILL LEAVE AN OPEN END ON THE DEATH SIDE, FOR IT IS NOT CERTAIN HOW LONG IT WILL TAKE TO SETTLE TO BUSINESS AND TAKE ON THOSE LESSONS WHICH ARE NECESSARY. THIS IS VERY RARE, HOWEVER. USUALLY THE TIME IS SET. THERE CAN BE AN EXTENSION IF THIS HAS BEEN ASKED FOR OR IS GREATLY NEEDED.

LH I think I'll ask for an extension. (She laughs.)

BH When an entity finds that the lessons he has contracted for are too overwhelming, and he can't bear with them, what are his alternatives?

S THIS ONE CAN CLOSE DOWN HIS CENTERS AND CLOSE SHOP, SO TO SPEAK. THIS OFTEN HAPPENS WITH THOSE WHO TRY TO EXCAPE THE WORLD OR BECOME RECLUSES. IT ALSO OCCURS WHEN ONE TRIES TO COMMIT SUICIDE OR LEAVE THE EARTH PLANE BECAUSE OF THE FEELING OF AN OVERWHELMING TASK.

IF THE ENTITY COULD REALIZE THAT ONLY THAT WHICH HE IS CAPABLE OF DOING HAS BEEN GIVEN TO HIM, HE WOULD THEN BE ABLE TO COPE WITH EACH PROBLEM AS IT ARISES, AND TAKE IT IN STRIDE INSTEAD OF TRYING TO SEE THE OVERALL PICTURE AND FEELING OVERWHELMED. IF HE WOULD ALSO RECOGNIZE THE FACT THAT THERE ARE MANY HELPERS—THOSE WHO WOULD GUIDE THE WAY AND GIVE HIM THE STRENGTH, IT WOULD MAKE HIS JOURNEY ON THE EARTH PLANE MUCH SIMPLER. HOWEVER, THESE ARE LESSONS THAT MAN, IN HIS OWN TIME, MUST LEARN.

BH Is suicide ever justified or forgiven without paying a heavy karmic debt?

S   THIS AGAIN DEPENDS UPON THE MOTIVE. THERE CAN BE
    TIMES WHEN SUICIDE IS NECESSARY FOR THAT PARTICULAR
    ENTITY TO LEAVE THE EARTH PLANE, FOR THE PROBLEMS
    HAVE BECOME SO OVERWHELMING THAT HE WOULD DO
    NOTHING BUT DETERIORATE FROM THAT POINT ON.

    IN THIS CASE, IT IS POSSIBLE THAT THE BODY BE RELEASED.
    THE SPIRIT, HOWEVER, DOES REMAIN NEAR THE EARTH FOR A
    TIME, AND IT CAUSES THAT ONE TO HAVE MORE DIFFICULTY
    IN TRYING TO WORK OUT THOSE PROBLEMS GIVEN TO IT.
    HOWEVER, IT DOES, IN TIME, REACH FORWARD.

    ONE WHO HAS BEEN SPIRITUALLY ENLIGHTENED ACCEPTS
    SUICIDE IN A BETTER MANNER, FOR IF HE TAKES HIS OWN
    LIFE HE IS AWARE THAT HE NEEDS TO LOOK FOR LIGHT
    HELPERS. HOWEVER, ONE WHO IS SPIRITUALLY ENLIGHTENED
    SELDOM DOES COMMIT THIS TYPE OF ACTION, EXCEPT IN
    CASES WHERE HE WOULD RELIEVE A PHYSICAL BURDEN ON
    OTHER MEMBERS OF THE FAMILY.

BH Can an entity subconsciously bring on a terminal
    disease such as cancer?

S   USUALLY THIS IS BROUGHT ON BY THE DETERIORATION OF
    THE EMOTIONS RATHER THAN A DESIRE TO BRING THIS ON.
    HOWEVER, ONE WHO HAS A STRONG DEATH WISH CAN BRING
    ON MANY FORMS OF ILLNESS OR HARM WITHOUT BEING CON-
    SCIOUSLY AWARE OF IT.

BH Does a mother who exercises her free will to abort pay a
    karmic debt?

S   SHE WILL MANY TIMES HAVE A GREAT DESIRE FOR CHILDREN
    IN A FUTURE LIFE AND NOT BE ABLE TO BEAR THEM.
    HOWEVER, THERE ARE ALSO TIMES WHEN THIS, TOO, IS
    FORGIVEN, DEPENDING ON THE NECESSITY AND THE TIMES
    THAT A SOUL CAN COME TO THE BODY THAT IS WITHIN THE
    BODY OF THE MOTHER AND BE RELEASED FOR FURTHER
    GROWTH—EVEN THOUGH IT IS ABORTED OR DOES NOT COME
    TO THAT PARTICULAR BODY.

IF THIS PARTICULAR BODY IS NOT MADE AVAILABLE, THAT SOUL MAY THEN CHOOSE OTHERS AND SOMETIMES AC-COMPLISH THE SAME PURPOSE.

BH Does the person or doctor who actually performs the abortion pay a karmic debt?

S AGAIN, DEPENDING ON THE MOTIVE. IF THIS DOCTOR DOES IT STRICTLY FOR THE MONEY OR THE GLORY INVOLVED, HE IS THEN RESPONSIBLE FOR ALL OF THESE DEATHS. IF HE IS DO-ING IT TO HELP HUMANITY, OR TO HELP A WOMAN WHO IS MENTALLY DISTURBED, HE IS NOT RESPONSIBLE AS A DEATH UPON HIS HANDS.

LH It feels that if his reasons are humane, this is not held against him.

Right after her children went to school we arrived at Lenora's to continue the inquiry.

With no sign of an ashtray, I hesitated to smoke in her house, but as the sessions lengthened, I asked her permission. Obligingly, she went to a cupboard and brought me one.

"You're welcome to smoke here," she smiled. "I just never think of it. Forgive me."

"Did you never smoke?" I asked.

"No, but I have another addiction: eating. As you can see, weight is a problem for me, and I consider the two, eating and smoking, as similar."

"You may be right," I agreed, and we both laughed at our human frailties.

A man with neither problem, Peter looked anxious for us to get through the small talk. In view of his first question, I felt the absurdity of our conversation.

PB Is there objective existence?

S   ONLY AS YOU DEEM IT TO BE NECESSARY. IT IS A VERY
    REAL . . .

LH It's like there should be words that I don't have, you
    know, and they aren't spelling them out for me, but it's
    like I'm using the wrong words, somehow.

S   IT IS A PROPERTY THAT IS VERY REAL IN THE TOTALITY OF
    THINGS. YOU WILL FIND THAT OBJECT REALITY IS THERE,
    AND YOU CAN TUNE INTO IT OR OUT OF IT. THIS IS MORE OF
    YOUR OWN DOING. IT IS NECESSARY THAT PEOPLE BECOME
    AWARE OF THE GOODNESS THAT IS AROUND THEM, OF THE
    REALITY THAT IS THERE. AND YET, THEY NEED NOT DEPEND
    ON IT AS THOUGH THE MATERIAL WERE A DEPENDABLE REALI-
    TY. THE REALITY IS MORE THAN WITHIN THE MIND OF THE
    MAKER, BUT THIS IS A STARTING POINT. THIS IS WHERE IT
    ALL BEGINS. AND YET, FROM THERE ON IT IS A REALITY AS
    EACH ENTITY CAN BE CONSIDERED REALITY, FOR ANYTHING
    YOU CAN PUT YOUR FINGER THROUGH IS NOT REALITY IN THE
    EYES OF MAN. AND YET THERE ARE MANY THINGS THAT HE
    CANNOT PUT HIS FINGER THROUGH THAT HE FEELS ARE
    REALITY.

PB What about subjective existence? Is there more than
    subjective existence?

S   THERE IS THE EXISTENCE THAT IS WITHIN AND THE EX-
    ISTENCE THAT IS WITHOUT. THERE ARE THE TWO TYPES OF
    EXISTENCE, AND THEY ARE NECESSARY TO EACH OTHER AND
    TO SUPPORT AND CONTAIN EACH OTHER. NEITHER IS TOTAL
    IN ITSELF. THEY MUST BE COMBINED TO CAUSE YOU TO KNOW
    THAT THIS IS MORE OF THE REALITY, AND YET THERE IS MORE
    BEYOND THIS. THERE IS SUPER . . .

LH Super something reality because these feel like steps.
    One feels like here and now and you. And one encom-
    passes you and takes more of that. But there seems to be
    even more beyond that.

PB Now I'm working on soul groups. Are you and my wife and I in the same soul group?

LH It says YES. And this seems to be spiritual level soul groups.

PB What about a smaller soul group?

LH A smaller soul group seems to be you, and goes through your family and some of your immediate friends, because it doesn't feel just all family.

PB Who is in my smaller soul group?

LH Well, your wife still feels to be. And I don't know which one, but it feels like one child, and I feel a brother-in-law, and then it seems to go to some close or dear friends. Do you have friends of 20 to 30 years standing?

PB Yes. This is within a very small soul group?

LH Yes. I don't know whether a Karma group is proper or not, but that feels more like a physical soul group . . . if there is such a thing.

PB Are there Karma groups?

S   YES.

LH I didn't know that. It was never asked before.

PB Do these Karma groups have similar Karmas to work out?

LH Not always, but when you say "Karma group" it feels like several Karma groups within a soul group. Some feel like just for benefit as far as encouragement goes, and some feel like benefit as far as working things out.

PB How many entities are there in the basic soul group?

LH Well, I get the number 1,000. I have no idea.

PB How many entities are there in the next-sized soul group?

LH This is more like 100,000.

PB But the Karma groups are small?

LH Yes, it feels like groups of ten.

PB And these are together physically?

LH Usually. It feels like most are together and a few come and go, but they always touch physically.

PB Is your guide in your basic soul group?

LH Yes, but here I have a feeling like a supervisor, like the one guide that is in my soul group would be over several within the same soul group.

PB To change subjects again, what must an entity on the spiritual level do to become manifested on the earth plane?

S   DESIRE IS THE MAIN MOTIVATOR HERE. HOWEVER THERE ARE SEVERAL REASONS FOR ENTITIES TO COME BACK TO THE EARTH PLANE. THEY CAN BE, IN A MANNER OF SPEAKING, TO HELP THAT PARTICULAR SOUL, FOR THEY CAN THEN VIEW THOSE SHORTCOMINGS OR AREAS OF NECESSITY THAT ARE STILL WITHIN THEM. THUS THEY CAN CHOOSE TO COME TO THE EARTH SO THAT THEY MIGHT DEVELOP THESE CHARAC-TERISTICS FURTHER, OR BECOME A BETTER OR MORE WHOLE BEING.

    THERE ARE THOSE WHO COME BACK BECAUSE OF GREED, WHO DESIRE TO GAIN A NAME FOR THEMSELVES, EVEN THOUGH THE NAME WOULD BE FLEETING IN THEIR TIME. THERE ARE THOSE THAT DESIRE TO INTRODUCE NEW IDEAS THAT HAVE BEEN ABLE TO BE DEVELOPED IN THE INTERIM TIME. THERE ARE THOSE WHO CHOOSE TO COME BACK THAT THEY MIGHT BE CHANNELS FOR HIGHER BEINGS, SO THAT THEY WILL HAVE AN OPEN VOICE UPON THE EARTH. THERE ARE THOSE WHO CHOOSE TO COME BACK SO THAT THEY MIGHT SERVE THEIR FELLOW MAN.

PB From life to life, why is the slate sometimes not wiped clean?

S THERE ARE TIMES WHEN THE HURT HAS BEEN SO DEEP THAT IT IS IMPOSSIBLE TO ERASE IT WITH JUST THE PASSING OVER INTO THE REALM. THIS IS A CASE IN WHICH MANY TIMES A CHILD NEEDS TO COME TO EARTH AGAIN JUST FOR THE RE-BIRTH EXPERIENCE SO THAT THIS CAN BE ACCOMPLISHED. MANY TIMES IT CAN BE LULLED, OR SOME SALVE PUT ON THE WOUND, SO THAT HEALING CAN THEN TAKE PLACE. MANY TIMES THE SLATE IS NOT WIPED CLEAN BECAUSE THERE NEEDS TO BE THIS REMNANT LEFT UPON THE EARTH SO THAT MAN MIGHT RECOGNIZE AND SEEK INTO THESE MATTERS, SO THAT HE WILL KNOW FROM WHENCE HE CAME, THAT THIS IS NOT A ONE-TIME EXPERIENCE, ONE IN WHICH HE CAN EITHER BE FOUND OR LOST, BUT ONE WHICH IS PART OF AN ON-GOING EXPERIENCE, ONE WHICH IS PART OF A TOTALITY.

THERE ARE ALSO TIMES WHEN THIS SO-CALLED SLATE IS LEFT PARTIALLY CLOSED OR CLOTTED, AND ONE IS LEFT WITH FAINT REMEMBRANCES OF EMOTIONS THAT ARE CARRIED OVER. THIS CAN ALSO CAUSE THEM TO PONDER MORE DEEPLY THE FACT OF PAST TIMES, THE FACT OF SHOULD I DO MORE WITH THIS PRESENT LIFE, THE FACT OF TRYING TO REACH OUT AND HELP OTHERS SO THAT THEY MIGHT OVERCOME MANY OF THESE BARRIERS. IT IS A VERY BENEFICIAL THING WHEN THIS HAS OCCURRED.

PB Could I recall manifestations that I experienced on other planets?

S YOU COULD, BUT NOTHING WOULD BE GAINED BY THIS, AND THUS IT IS A DIFFICULT TASK FOR YOU TO CARRY THROUGH.

LH It feels like diligent work would be able to pin it down, but it goes down like a pinpoint of light into total darkness.

PB Does an entity have recall of all earth incarnations while in the between-stage?

S   Usually only the more beneficial aspects of a particular experience will come forth. If he is one who is diligently seeking, he would be able to recall any and all experiences. However, the . . .

LH It looks like a graph or a scale, and he seems to be able to quickly tune or skim across the top, so these high points or important points are all that show. But the rest is all there.

PB Are we incarnating from life to life only on the earth level at this time?

S   At this particular period, yes. There are a few on earth that have come from other planets, and they would be able to return there more readily than you who have been so long away from your own planet.

PB From what planet did I come?

LH I seem to be getting . . . you are a . . . I feel like I am getting Uranus, but I'm not sure if it's possible that people have been there.

PB Let's ask! Do we come from planets outside our solar system?

S   Yes.

PB Will we go back?

S   You will go on.

PB To other solar systems?

S   Yes, there are galaxies and galaxies and solar systems and solar systems.

PB Do we have a series of earth incarnations which would be a life experience?

LH Yes, and what I see . . . apparently it represents a whole solar system . . . is a series of bubbles, the way a bubble bath looks. And when you say "will we go back" it feels like always onward. Now, where onward is, I have no idea.

PB A series of life incarnations on earth and then you do a series of life incarnations on another planet or in another solar system?

LH Yes. You feel like you hit several planets here in one solar . . . I don't know what a solar system represents . . . or a universe . . . or a galaxy. Anyway, there are several different areas with many lives on each one in one bubble. And then I progress to another, and there seems to be the same type of experience. It feels five or six, maybe seven different planets and several lives on each.

PB We've had experience on Venus and Mars?

S Yes.

PB Do you have life on the sun?

LH I've never asked. All right, it says . . .

S A TYPE OF LIFE OR EXISTENCE THAT IS A NON-PHYSICAL EXISTENCE, BUT A VERY CONSCIOUS ONE, ONE WHICH IS VERY ENERGIZING, ONE WHICH GIVES A PERSON THE IMPETUS TO MOVE FORWARD.

LH It feels like first stop. And I gather energy there and then start out on . . .

PB It's the first stop?

S Yes.

PB And then the other planets?

S YES, FOR THEN YOU ARE MORE ABLE TO TAKE ON A PHYSICAL BEING IN THESE PARTICULAR AREAS—PHYSICAL IN HOW THAT PARTICULAR PLANET RECOGNIZES PHYSICAL. AND

THROUGH THIS, YOU CAN GO THROUGH THE DIFFERENT LEVELS OF GROWTH THAT ARE NECESSARY. AS YOU LEAVE THIS PARTICULAR UNIVERSE, OR BUBBLE, EVERYTHING FEELS VERY MUCH REPEATED. NOT EXACTLY REPEATED, BUT ON A HIGHER PLANE. SO IT IS ALWAYS A HIGHER PLANE.

LH No one seems to actually regress unless they go back to help.

PB Describe in detail how we, in an earth-manifested incarnation, can discover the level of our spiritual progress on the scale of our specific soul. Give me a measure, such as a meter, and tell me at what level I am if my ultimate objective were 100 and I started at zero.

(Once again Peter, who used graphs and charts in his business life, turned to figures for a clarification.)

LH All right. You feel 78, whatever that means. And I get it in degrees.

S YOU WILL FIND THAT THIS REPRESENTS A GREATER THAN HALF PROGRESS THROUGH YOUR TOTAL LIVES WITHIN THIS BUBBLE, AND THAT YOU ARE JUST POLISHING MANY OF THE THINGS THAT ARE WITH YOU. YOU WILL FIND THAT THE LAST 25% OR DEGREES ARE THOSE THAT MOVE VERY RAPIDLY. THE FIRST 25 DEGREES ARE THOSE WHICH ARE VERY DIFFICULT OR SLOW FOR A PERSON TO SHOW.

THIS IS WHY MANY PEOPLE ON THE EARTH PLANE APPEAR TO BE ALMOST ANIMALISTIC IN THEIR APPROACH TO THINGS. THERE ARE MANY WHO APPEAR ALMOST AS VEGETABLES. YOU WILL FIND THAT THIS IS THE MOST DIFFICULT TIME. THE NEXT 25 DEGREES ARE MUCH MORE RAPID IN THEIR PROGRESS, BUT THEY ARE ALSO VERY DIFFICULT PHYSICALLY, AS A RULE. THE NEXT 25 POINTS ARE MORE EASY AND ARE MANIFESTED BY PEOPLE WITH AN EXTREME CURIOSITY, AS A RULE.

YOU WILL ALSO FIND THAT THE LAST 25 DEGREES MOVE VERY RAPIDLY, AS THERE IS MUCH TO BUILD ON AT THAT POINT. THIS IS USUALLY THE SPIRITUAL REALM AND ONE IN

WHICH A PERSON CAN PROGRESS RAPIDLY, FOR HE IS ALSO ABLE TO REACH OUT INTO THE SPIRIT REALM AND CAN DRAW HELP TO HIMSELF.

PB Are the more primitive-type peoples on a lower level in this sense?

S AS A RULE. HOWEVER, THERE ARE THOSE WHO HAVE VOLUNTEERED TO GO BACK INTO THOSE AREAS AND HELP RAISE THE LEVEL OF THINKING. BE AWARE THAT EVEN THOUGH A PERSON APPEARS TO BE MORE PRIMITIVE IN HIS PARTICULAR AREA, HE MAY BE ONE THAT HAS DEVELOPED A SENSE OF WORTH, OR REALITY, OF FAIRNESS, OF EQUALITY. AND THESE ARE CHARACTERISTICS THAT ARE NECESSARY.

(This seemed a good warning to all of us who might feel superior to those on lower rungs of the ladder.)

PB Do we go all the way from zero to 100 on this scale on earth here now?

S YES. BUT WHEREAS IT MAY TAKE 100 MORE INCARNATIONS TO MANIFEST THE FIRST TEN POINTS, IT MAY TAKE ONLY THREE TO DO THE LAST 25 POINTS, SO THIS IS NOT SOMETHING YOU CAN GAUGE BY.

LH In the first I feel like I'm bogged down in mud, and I just can't pull myself out of it, and it feels very slow . . . like falling slow motion.

PB The incarnations we hear most about occurred in Atlantis, Egypt, the Roman Empire, the Middle Ages, etc. Where were we during the other periods?

S THERE HAVE BEEN MANY LIVES SUCH AS THOSE OF THE CAVE DWELLERS, THOSE OF THE EARLY INDIANS, THOSE OF THE LOST-SEEMING SOULS THAT ARE SELDOM MENTIONED, FOR THESE ARE NOT IMPORTANT LIVES TO THE AVERAGE SOUL IN HIS PARTICULAR PROGRESS. HOWEVER, IF ONE WERE TO MAKE A LIFE-TO-LIFE EXPERIENCE DRAWING, HE WOULD FIND

THAT ALL OF THESE COME FORTH. EACH ONE HAS BEEN ALL THINGS AT ONE TIME OR ANOTHER, EVEN TO THE LOWEST OF CAVEMEN, EVEN TO THE HIGHEST OF THE PATRIARCHS.

PB   In other words, these particular historic periods are the ones that have been most productive?

LH   Yes, and I get the word "CATACLYSMIC."

(Now, *that's* a word that can reach into all our hearts.)

PB   Describe the various life forms that are self-conscious.

S   ANIMALS IN THEIR MORE EVOLVED FORMS ARE SELF-CON-SCIOUS. MANKIND, OF COURSE. PLANT LIFE AS IT RELATES TO ITSELF.

LH   And by that, it feels like a plant does if it knows an animal is going to eat it, or a human being is going to break it. Then it is aware. If it's in a forest where all is peace and quiet, then it doesn't seem to be self-conscious.

PB   Isn't that interesting?

LH   If true. I don't feel that birds are. I can't tell. It feels more instinct than self-conscious. Dogs seem to be. Animals . . . well, there again, more when they relate to a higher form. This seems to be when they are more self-conscious. When they are with their own kind again, it feels like they then rely more on instinct.

PB   Do animals have souls?

LH   It says DO BIRDS HAVE WINGS?

S   YES, ANIMALS HAVE SOULS, BUT THEY ARE NOT THAT TYPE WHICH BECOMES A HUMAN SOUL. THEY HAVE THEIR OWN REALM AND UNIVERSE AND PURPOSE. THIS IS NOT TO BE CONFUSED WITH THE HUMAN SOUL, BUT IT IS A VERY REAL ONE NEVERTHELESS.

PB Do insects have souls?

S   OF A TYPE. IT IS MORE OF A GROUP SOUL.

PB Do fish have souls?

S   THEY DON'T WEAR SHOES.

(At this we all burst out laughing at the unexpected humor.)

LH Fish feel in this group soul thing.

PB Plants?

S   NOT AS YOU DESCRIBE OR DEFINE A SOUL, NO. PLANTS HAVE
    A LIFE OR BEING, AND THEY ARE PART OF THE CAPITAL A ALL-
    IN-ALL.

LH But they don't seem to have souls.

PB How about minerals and chemicals?

LH It just says "THEY ARE" and Are is capitalized.

PB Each atom, though, has . . .

S   CONSCIOUSNESS.

PB Now, does each soul continue to reincarnate in the same
    life form on a given planet? For example, dog to dog,
    etc?

S   YES, EXCEPT THAT . . .

LH There seem to be groups, for instance dog-wolf, and
    animals that are the same line like cats and tigers. Now,
    they seem to fluctuate back and forth between that, but
    not between cat to dog to ape.

PB Do these souls then go through other life forms on other
    planets?

S   YES, WITHIN THEIR OWN NEED. THEY DO NOT HAVE THE
    SAME NEED AS A HUMAN SOUL. THEY DO NOT EVOLVE TO THE

STRENGTH OR THE SCOPE OF A HUMAN SOUL, BUT THEY DO
EVOLVE TO OTHER PLANETS. THEY SERVE A PURPOSE.

PB   Can animal life be sustained with the body and the spirit
     alone? Without soul?

S   No. THERE NEED NOT BE AN AWARENESS OF SOUL, BUT
     THERE NEEDS TO BE THAT WHICH IS ATTACHED TO THE BODY
     OR IS THE OVERSEER OF ALL. THIS IS THE SOUL. THIS IS
     ATTACHED.

PB   Thank you, Lenora, and to your Source. We are going
     back to British Columbia to find a place to live, so we
     won't see you for a few weeks when we return on busi-
     ness. But then I'd like to finish the last series of
     questions.

LH   Of course. I'd be glad to work with you any time. Have
     a good trip!

Before we met again we had an amazing experience. Our
friends who introduced us to Vancouver Island invited us to
dinner to meet a new friend of theirs. "We think he'll interest
you," they said. "He owns the local Sealand and has just
become the proud new owner of the only white whale in
captivity."

CHAPTER 4

Psychic Sensitives

Lenora when we next met was delighted by our discovery of the white whale which proved amusingly that we were somehow operating on a scheduled outline for our growth.

Peter told her this would be our last series of questions and would concern how psychic sensitives operate.

"Fine," said Lenora. "If you are comfortable and ready, let's begin."

PB How does your source communicate with you?

S   THERE HAS BEEN THE NEED HERE FOR A LONG, SLOW PROCESS, ONE IN WHICH THE CONSCIOUS MIND OF THIS ONE HAS BEEN SOOTHED OR QUIETED SO THAT MORE THINGS ARE NOW ABLE TO COME THROUGH. THIS IS A MIND-TO-MIND CONTACT. ONE IN WHICH THOUGHTS ARE SENT OUT ON VIBRATIONS OR WAVE LENGTHS AND THESE ARE . . .

LH The picture I'm seeing is like my mind goes up like a receiving tower and they hit that and then come down.

S   THERE ARE TIMES WHEN THIS ONE IS NOT OPEN TO SUGGESTIONS THAT COME. IT IS THEN GIVEN IN A DIFFERENT FORM

SUCH AS THROUGH THE WRITING. THIS IS ONLY WHEN IT IS
OF A DEEPER NATURE, AND THE CHANNEL IS NOT YET SURE
THAT SHE CAN RECEIVE CLEARLY OR PURELY ON THIS SUB-
JECT. THIS IS WHEN SHE REVERTS TO WRITING.

PB   Are these vibrations alpha or theta or what specifically?

LH   It's going like this. (She draws horizontal parallel lines.)
And when I get down here, it's deep purple. Alpha
seems to be up here, and when I keep going deeper and
deeper and deeper, this seems like it's deep purple. That
isn't an answer.

PB   Is that theta?

LH   That doesn't fit on it. It seems to be something that
starts with an O or an Oph.

PB   Is it at four meters?

LH   No. What is at 5.6? Does that mean anything at all?

PB   It is 5.6 meters?

S   YES.

PB   Is it 5.6 millimeters?

LH   Would that be the same as micrometers? Micro-
something.

PB   Microwaves?

S   YES.

PB   5.6 microwaves. I have no idea what microwaves are,
but I suspect we'll discover they exist. Now, for further
clarification, is your guide or master actually drawing
on the entity's subconscious mind when he answers our
questions? In other words, is your master drawing on
your vocabulary and your subconscious thinking?

S   No, BUT IT MUST COME THROUGH WORDS THAT ARE
FAMILIAR OR USABLE THROUGH THIS CHANNEL . . . IT MUST

COME THROUGH WORDS THAT SHE CAN COMPREHEND OR UN-
DERSTAND OR CAN PUT A VARIETY OF FEELING WITH. IT MUST
COME IN TERMS THAT CAN BE USED BY HER.

PB These terms are not bouncing back, though, to the
source? The source is developing its own terms?

LH It says NO.

PB Is it using my thought to answer my questions?

LH With that it says, NOT USUALLY.

S THERE IS THE ANSWER COMING FROM THE ULTIMATE
SOURCE, FROM THAT WHICH YOU BOTH DRAW ON, FROM
THAT WHICH IS COMMON BETWEEN YOU, BUT IT IS NEITHER
YOURS NOR HERS. IT IS NEITHER HERE NOR THERE.

PB O.K., now, the reason I ask, and you might think about
this for a moment to see where it comes in, is: I'm wondering if I'm just reflecting my own thinking. In other
words, I'm asking the questions in such a way that it's
answering what either I want to hear, or something of
this type.

LH It says NO.

S YOU ARE ASKING BECAUSE OF THE WISDOM THAT'S WITHIN
YOU. YOU ARE ABLE TO FORM AND PHRASE THOSE THOUGHTS
WHICH NEED TO BE PUT DOWN, WHICH NEED TO BE HEARD,
AND YET IT IS NECESSARY THAT YOU DO THIS IN A CONSCIOUS
WAY. THROUGH THIS YOU ARE THEN, MANY TIMES, ABLE TO
ANSWER YOUR OWN QUESTIONS, FOR YOU ARE ALSO RECEIV-
ING ON A LEVEL THAT YOU ARE NOT FULLY AWARE OF AS YET.

PB Is it necessary for a psychic sensitive to be aware of the
material that he is passing on?

S ONLY TO THE EXTENT THAT THEY WILL BE ABLE TO IDENTIFY
THE PICTURES THAT COME OR FORM THE WORDS THAT ARE
GIVEN.

LH   For instance, if one is unable to mouth a certain sound, it feels that then they cannot say that word. By that, it feels like if they don't know the language, they can make the sound that is nearest to it. But they could do it while in trance without being . . . yes. Then all the conscious nerves are set to one side, and I'm seeing a marionette as though someone else can pull the strings.

PB   Is this a more desirable way for a psychic channel to work?

S   DEPENDING ON THE NEED, THE NEED FOR CLARITY, THE NEED FOR PURENESS, THE NEED TO SET ONE'S SELF ASIDE. IT IS NOT A FLAT NECESSITY. HOWEVER, IT CAN BE VERY BENEFICIAL TO MANY.

PB   In thinking of spiritually-sensitive people, are these people like a tube that goes through a wall into a lighted room, and only that light coming through the tube can come out as a narrow beam—therefore each tube is completely separate and there is no purpose in bringing them together?

LH   No, because even as you talk I feel several pieces of macaroni or tubes being placed side by side and then the beam, instead of being straight ahead, seems to fan out. Like instead of this spot and this spot, like that, but when they are put together they seem to cover not only these spots but the light of it goes out even further.

S   THERE IS A GREAT DEAL OF MISUNDERSTANDING WITH THOSE THAT ARE IN THIS FIELD, THOSE WHO ARE CONSIDERED SENSITIVE, FOR THEY ARE VERY NARROW. THEY ARE AFRAID OF BEING THREATENED BY OTHERS WHO MAY RECEIVE TRUTH EVEN HIGHER THAN THEIRS, OR TRUTH WHICH COULD CONTRADICT SOMETHING WHICH THEY HAVE ALREADY RECEIVED. THEY HAVE THE SENSE OF NOT FULLY UNDERSTANDING OR COMPREHENDING THE VARYING DEGREES OF THAT WHICH

WOULD REACH BEYOND WHAT THEY SAY. THEY NEED TO EN-
VELOP ALL THAT IS SAID BY ONE AND THE OTHER SO THAT
THEY CAN COMBINE THIS AND GET A FULLER MEANING TO
THOSE THINGS WHICH NEED TO BE GIVEN.

PB Can a group of spiritual sensitives become a clearer
channel or become more effective than an individual?

S NOT MORE EFFECTIVE IN THEIR MANNER OF PRAYER. THEY
MAY BE MORE EFFECTIVE IN THAT THEY CAN HEAR OR SENSE
THE ANSWER. THIS WOULD BE THE ONLY ADVANTAGE THERE.

PB Can some people, in fact, communicate with those who
have passed on?

S YES. THIS GOES ON TO A GREAT EXTENT, FOR THERE ARE
MANY WHO ARE ABLE TO SEE OR TO HEAR. THERE ARE MANY
WHO ARE ABLE TO FEEL THE PRESENCE OF THOSE WHO HAVE
GONE ON. AND YET THE COMMUNICATION IS NOT ALWAYS
THE SAME.

THERE ARE TIMES WHEN CERTAIN WORDS ARE POINTED
OUT IN A BOOK THAT THE DECEASED ONE WOULD CALL TO
THIS PERSON'S ATTENTION.

THERE ARE TIMES WHEN THERE IS ALMOST LIKE A
WHISPERING IN THE EAR, AND THERE ARE OTHER TIMES THAT
IT IS JUST A KNOWING THAT THE PRESENCE IS THERE. HOW-
EVER, THE COMMUNICATION CAN TAKE PLACE IN MANY
FORMS, AND IT IS NOT ALWAYS A SIGN OR SYMBOL THAT ONE
IS TRULY HEALTHY OR READY TO GO ON.

IT IS IMPORTANT THAT THEY NOT BE CALLED UNLESS THEY
ARE READY TO MAKE CONTACT, FOR THERE ARE TIMES THAT
THEY ARE BUSY WITH THEIR OWN WORK. THERE ARE ALSO
TIMES THAT THEY ARE NOT OF THE STRENGTH THAT IS SUFFI-
CIENT FOR THEM TO BE ABLE TO COME BACK INTO THE VIBRA-
TION OF THE EARTH. THESE THINGS HAVE A GREAT FLUX IN
THEM AS FAR AS BEING ABLE TO LAY DOWN CERTAIN LAWS.

LH Yes, is the answer to your question.

PB Can those entities be on any level of the spirit world, or must they be at a between-stage to be communicated with?

S   No. THE BETWEEN-STAGE IS ONE WHICH IS YET LIKE A VEIL AROUND THE SPIRIT. THEY ARE NOT ABLE TO SEE BEYOND AND REALIZE THAT WHICH THEY ARE NOT TOUCHING. AND YET, THERE ARE THOSE WHO HAVE REACHED A HIGHER PLANE OF CONSCIOUSNESS THAT CAN COME BACK TO THE EARTH. THESE ARE THE ONES WHICH TAKE MORE ENERGY OR POWER BE-CAUSE THEY MUST LOWER THEIR VIBRATION TO BE ABLE TO COMMUNICATE. THEY DO NOT MAKE THE CONTACT AS OFTEN. THEIR GUIDANCE OR HELP IS MORE GENERAL AND NOT AS SPECIFIC, AS A RULE. KNOW THAT THEY ARE ABLE TO SEE THE AREAS WHERE STRUGGLE MUST BE MADE, AND THEY ARE WILLING TO ALLOW OTHERS TO GO ON.

LH There seem to be levels where they can no longer con-tact the earth, but they don't seem to desire to. They feel like they can contact down on, say, one or two levels and this, in turn, can come down. It's like a relay. They can send messages if they want, but they don't seem to desire to particularly.

PB Is there any constructive reason to communicate with those who have passed through the door called Death?

S   ONLY BY A MANNER OF REASSURANCE, EITHER TO THOSE WHO ARE YET ON THE EARTH PLANE OR THOSE WHO HAVE PASSED THROUGH AND DO NOT UNDERSTAND THE REASON FOR THEIR PASSING AS YET. IT IS A REASSURANCE. THIS IS ALL.

PB When guides and such read the future, are they, in fact, making projections on the Akashic Records?

S   THEY ARE PROJECTING FROM THOSE THINGS WHICH APPEAR TO BE. HOWEVER, THEY ARE ALSO AWARE THAT THERE CAN BE AN ABOUT-FACE OR CHANGE WITHIN THE WILL OF THE

ONE WHO HAS BEEN GIVEN THE INFORMATION. THEY ARE ALSO AWARE THAT BY PLANTING THE THOUGHT, THIS MANY TIMES BRINGS IT ABOUT, FOR ONE FEELS THIS IS PREDETERMINED.

LH And I'm seeing it more like guidelines than definite.

PB What is the margin of error due to free will?

LH It feels like ten percent.

PB What other factors can cause error?

LH Again it feels like the interpretation.

S YOU WILL FIND THAT MANY OF THE THINGS WHICH HAVE BEEN PROJECTED WILL COME ABOUT, BUT IN A DIFFERENT MANNER THAN HAS BEEN EXPECTED. THOSE WORDS WHICH HAVE BEEN PUT UPON THESE THINGS ARE MANY TIMES NOT AS CLEAR AS THE PICTURE HAS BEEN. KNOW THAT THE FORM OF COMMUNICATION AND THE SEMANTIC PROBLEM WITHIN THE WORLD CAUSE A GREAT DEAL OF FALLACY.

PB When consulting with a psychic or spiritual sensitive, how does one know that this channel is, in fact, tuned into Universal Mind?

S ONLY TO THE EXTENT THAT YOU ARE ABLE TO LISTEN WITH YOUR INNER EAR. AS YOU FEEL THE TRUTH, THERE IS A REVERBERATION TO IT SO THAT YOU CAN RECOGNIZE THE VALIDITY. THIS IS NOT SOMETHING THAT CAN COME QUICKLY. YOU CANNOT SAY, "AH, YES, THIS ONE IS TUNED IN, OR THIS ONE IS NOT."

LH It's more like in the overall picture I can get bits and pieces and then tell.

PB How can one best learn to read or communicate with those spirits one wishes to communicate with?

S IT DEPENDS UPON YOUR MODE OF OPERATION. IF YOU CARE TO USE A PENCIL OR A LISTENING TIME, THESE ARE TWO OF

THE MOST AVAILABLE. THE OUIJA BOARD CAN BE USED. HOW-
EVER, THIS CAN BE ONE OF THE LOWER FORMS. KNOW THAT
THIS CAN BE VERY VALID.

PB How can one best protect against being possessed by a
discarnate spirit?

S SEEK NOT TO CONTACT THE SPIRIT WORLD UNTIL YOU ARE
READY TO SEEK SPIRITUAL PROGRESS AND TO MOVE TO
HIGHER REALMS. WHEN YOU ARE DOING THIS THROUGH A
MATTER OF CURIOSITY, OR YOU ARE DOING THINGS WHICH
CAUSE YOUR BODY TO BE AT A LESS HEALTHY OR STABLE
PLACE, YOU WILL FIND THAT THIS, TOO, ALLOWS THE EN-
TRANCE OF A DISCARNATE SPIRIT. KEEP YOUR MIND
GUARDED AT ALL TIMES.

LH And I'm feeling like . . . not a wire fence . . . a barbed
wire fence. And it feels like if you keep this fence up
with the electricity going through the wire, you don't
need to worry.

PB Keep your vibrations up?

LH Right. And your thoughts or emotions. Everything high
or positive or . . . I get tired of the term 'upwards,' but
this always implies spiritual. Keep everything on an up
plane. And it feels like even if you're in a negative
mood, then try to repeat positive things, whether you
believe them or not at the time.

PB Why did Edgar Cayce go into a hypnotic trance to give
his readings?

S HE WAS OF A NATURE THAT THIS WAS QUITE NECESSARY. HE
WAS ONE THAT WOULD HAVE REFUSED TO OPEN HIS MOUTH
HAD IT NOT COME THROUGH IN AN UNCONSCIOUS FORM. IT
WAS NECESSARY FOR HIM TO BE HIT OVER THE HEAD SO THAT
HE WOULD BE MORE READILY AVAILABLE. HOWEVER, HIS UN-
CONSCIOUS MIND WAS ONE THAT WAS VERY PURE AND ALSO

ONE THAT WAS CLEAR FOR A CHANNEL. THIS WAS A BEAUTI-
FUL USE OF ONE OF THE GIFTS OF TIME.

PB Let's assume here that you are reading a past life. Are
you reading the Akashic Records of that past life, or are
you reading the individual spirit?

LH I don't know. All right. This says, The AKASHIC RECORD.

S THE AKASHIC RECORD AS INTERPRETED THROUGH THAT
SPIRIT WHICH IS STANDING NEAR. HOWEVER, WHEN YOU
READ THE PAST LIVES OF OTHERS WHO ARE NOT PRESENT,
THIS IS READING THE RECORD THAT IS WITHIN THE ETHERS
AND NOT DIVULGED THROUGH THE SPIRIT.

PB Is the person that does the reading able to differentiate?
Does he know what he's reading?

S NOT ALWAYS.

PB Not generally even?

LH I guess not, if you're asking me. No.

PB Can anyone read or communicate with these past
spirits?

S IF THE NEED IS THERE AND THE CENTERS ARE DEVELOPED SO
THAT THEY ARE SENSITIVE TO THESE PARTICULAR BEINGS OR
VIBRATIONS, YES.

PB When someone reads past lives, are they, in fact,
reading the spirit of that entity in *that* life?

S NOT AS SUCH. BUT IT WOULD APPEAR THIS WAY MANY
TIMES, FOR MANY OF THE CHARACTERISTICS WHICH COME
FORTH WITH A PERSON ARE THOSE THINGS WHICH HAVE BEEN
ABLE TO IDENTIFY IN PAST LIVES. THESE ARE ALSO TRAITS
WHICH COME FORTH. BUT THERE ARE TIMES THAT A PAR-
TICULAR TRAIT FROM ONE LIFE WILL BE TOTALLY REVERSED
IN ANOTHER. THIS CAN BE AN ATTITUDE TOWARD CERTAIN

THINGS, AND YOU WILL FIND THAT THIS DOES NOT ALWAYS
CARRY THROUGH AS AN ONGOING THING.

LH Did that make it clear?

PB If someone is regressed to his past life, does his present
mind, in fact, join that past spirit so that he feels that he
is, in fact, living that previous life?

S   YES.

With this Peter came to the end of his questions. We all
looked at each other, breathing a joint sigh of relief. And yet
at the same time I felt regret that it was over.

"Thank you very much," Peter said to Lenora, "for all
your time and care in seeing this through. And thank you to
your 'source' who has given us this gift."

"And thank YOU," she answered, "for I have enjoyed this
experience more than any of the other questions that are
brought to me. I recall that each time we did this, there was
such a feeling of awe about the situation."

"Yes, it is wonderful material," I added.

Lenora stopped us.

"Before you leave, I'd like to ask my 'source' about you
both. This is a special gift for you."

LH Who is Peter Boulton?

S   HE IS ONE WHO HAS FREED HIMSELF OF MANY KARMIC EN-
TANGLEMENTS AND HAS DEVELOPED HIS OWN SENSE OF
WORTH AND IDENTITY. HE IS ONE WHO IS ABLE TO MOVE
MOUNTAINS WHEN PROPERLY MOTIVATED. HE HAS A WILL
AND A TEMPERAMENT THAT ARE DESIGNED AND DESIGNATED
TO ACCOMPLISH! GIVEN THE TIME, HE HAS THE ABILITY AND
AVAILABLE ASSETS TO HELP HIS FELLOW MAN IN MANY WAYS.
HE WILL FIND THAT HE IS VERY DRAWN TO THE ENVIRON-
MENTAL ECOLOGY PROBLEM IN A FEW YEARS. HE IS A CHOSEN
SON OF THE COSMOS, BUT ONLY AS HE SO CHOOSES AND

DEIGNS TO FOLLOW HIS GUIDANCE WILL HE FEEL THE GLORY OF THIS DESCENDING UPON HIM. HE IS CHOSEN ONLY IN THAT HE SO CHOOSES TO FOLLOW A POSITIVE PATH OF AD-VANCEMENT AND SEEKS TO DEFINE PURPOSE OF BEING. HE WILL FIND THAT THIS IS NOT AS A BURDEN, BUT AS AN EX-CITING JOY TO HIM. WHO IS HE? HE IS ONE AND ALL, WITH-IN HIMSELF COMPLETE AND PARTIAL—A BEING OF WORTH, OF DESIRE, OF NEED, OF GIVINGNESS. HE IS!

LH Who is Jane Boulton?

S   SHE IS ONE OF COMPASSION, OF UNDERSTANDING, OF SENSI-TIVITY. WHO IS THIS CHILD? ONE WHO WOULD WANT TO MOVE MOUNTAINS, BUT WILL PLANT THE IDEAS WITH HER HUSBAND. SHE IS ONE OF A DREAMER'S SOUL—IDEALISTIC—SEEING ALL THINGS AS NEEDING HELP AND WANTING TO GIVE IN A SELFLESS WAY. THERE IS HEALING IN HER THOUGHTS AND MERCY IN HER JUDGMENT. THIS ONE IS A BLESSING TO HER HUSBAND AND A VERY WELL-BALANCED PARTNER FOR HIM. SHE IS AS THE ANCHOR TO THE SHIP AND YET DOES NOT WEIGH HEAVILY. SHE IS ALSO AS A RUDDER, WHILE HE IS THE STRENGTH THAT GUIDES THROUGH ALL THE STORMS. SHE IS A DELICATE, NOT A WEAK, SOUL THAT WAFTS THROUGH THIS SPHERE ON A MISSION OF LOVE, MERCY AND BALANCE. SHE IS MANY TIMES HURT TO THE QUICK BY THOSE WHO WOULD BLUNDER PAST HER IN THE RUSH OF LIFE, BUT SHE DOES NOT CRUMPLE UNDER THE ONSLAUGHT. SHE HOLDS HER PLACE AND CONTINUES ON. MUCH OF THE GOOD SHE AC-COMPLISHES IS IN A SILENT, UNSUNG WAY. SHE IS A SOUL PASSING THROUGH THIS SCENE AIMED TOWARD PERFECTION—STRIVING, WORKING, FLOWING FORWARD. SO BE IT.

Postscript

Consulting A Psychic Sensitive

Peter Boulton

There is, as we've learned, a master computer in the universe which records all experiences of mankind—each event, thought, word and emotion. Frequently referred to as the Akashic Records, Edgar Cayce called it "a vibratory record of all thought and action." It is like a photo plate from which no occurrence can be hidden. Any bits of information can be taken from the Akashic Records if one is able to contact the various beings in the spirit world having access to this universal file.

It is like having information ten million years old available with instant replay. Time, space and distance do not exist for this purpose. In fact, since other levels of consciousness are bound by our earth concept of time, those tuning in to their levels are easily able to read on the past or the future.

A person able to transmit these various phenomena may be known by the name of prophet, seer, medium, psychic sensitive, channel or receiving station. Because they are drawing thoughts from psychic sources, I prefer the term "psychic sensitive."

They may read the spirit of another person (dead or alive by earth thinking) or the soul or the Karma or the Akashic Records. This is still to be determined by future investigations. Since each of these phenomena exist at different levels, a psychic must function at the vibratory level where he has the facility, explaining why some people can read different things than others.

This tuning skill may be likened to listening to a radio or viewing television in that first there must be a power source for sending and then power for the received, tuning in to a compatible wave length. It can also be pictured as a stroboscope or electric fan. If the light is flashing a certain number of times per minute (the frequency) in time with the fan blades, you can see the blades as though they were standing still. Otherwise they are just a blur.

Finding a psychic sensitive is an individual demonstration. Most often they are advertised by a word-of-mouth process for the people discussing these matters. The Association for Research and Enlightenment, which evolved from Edgar Cayce's work in the field of parapsychology, has dicussion groups that meet in many cities. They may be contacted at P.O. Box 595, Virginia Beach, Virginia 23451 where they have gathered material covering the full range of psychic studies. As a member, you will be sent their reading lists and will be told where the group meets that is nearest you.

Another source is bookstores specializing in esoteric materials (metaphysical, occult) which stock books listing talented psychic sensitives.

In London is the famous Spiritualist Association of Great Britain, 33 Belgrave Square, London SW 1, where they will make an appointment for you right there in their offices as though you were seeing a doctor.

As a test to your own powers, I suggest that readers wanting to learn more of the subject simply know they will be led to the right sources for their own needs.

Once you have found a sensitive to read for you, be sure to take along a tape recorder (asking permission first) in order that the session may be accurately preserved. It is astonishing to learn how much clearer it is, with perhaps other meanings, than during the time you were recording.

The simplest method is to ask a direct question, either orally or mentally, trusting that the "source" will receive it as intended. In this regard, it is important to have the question carefully thought out in advance. Ambiguous questions, I have found, lead to confused answers.

Aware that thoughts and feelings make impressions on particularly sensitive people, I try to guard my own thinking that it may not cause interference. For this reason, I schooled myself over the months of taping not to respond to answers as they came but to wait for a replay of the tape to review and evaluate. A further refinement was to write each question on a separate card, looking at that question only as it came up.

These psychically gifted ones have occasionally discovered their gift through their own searching, while others were influenced by forces outside themselves to act as channels. Even some unbelievers have been groomed by those on other levels, surprised to have messages coming through them, reluctant to have their lives taken over from entirely different careers.

Once psychics start to receive communications, they tend to develop their own techniques that work for them in reading at consultations. Although automatic writing and psychometry are quite common, the techniques used are amazingly varied. Many psychics are able to receive information simply by being in the presence of the questioner, pouring out facts to him about his life in its many aspects.

Others, like Lenora Huett, work by answering only the questions put to them.

Astrology, reading cards, numerology, graphology, palm reading and Tarot cards are useful vehicles for some psychics, serving as a kind of handle. These various esoteric disciplines, each having value in its own right, act as catalysts to assist sensitives in being effective.

It is interesting to observe their systems for reading—similar to an astrologer who goes around the chart dealing with each house representing a different department of life. Often a sensitive will read on your family, frequently picking up on dead relatives. This proves, first of all, that he is reading clairvoyantly, and secondly, establishes that he is reading on YOU. (If he does not establish that you are the subject, there is no point in continuing the session.) From the opening position he may proceed to your job, money, health etc.

At some point in my research I decided against hearing any more from my dead relatives. Then it came to me that if the guide or source has access to all information that exists in the universe, he should be able to get my thoughts and intention. Before a reading I listed my questions, meditating on them prior to my appointment. No matter how far ahead I worked this out it was effective. A sensitive would start reading in his or her usual manner and then would say, "Wait . . . they are telling me to skip that and go on to . . ."

Words are important in this, as in every other, field of communication—difficult because of personal meanings or emotions they evoke. Psychics can be restricted by their own reactions, and since they are our translators, we must be aware of this problem in determining the extent of accuracy.

In covering the questions of this book, it became increasingly clear how lacking our language is in vocabulary for our understanding. For the field of psychic explorations we will need many new words.

Frank Lloyd Wright, a genius in architecture, loved to invent words. A musician friend, Robert Erickson, coined the word "audiolize" as related to music rather than visualize (what the deaf Beethoven could do). Heinline created the word "grok." Overstreet invented "empathy."

As our vocabularies expand, communications from the other side will also expand and become more clear through the channels.

How clearly a psychic receives depends, in part also, on how well he can keep himself out of the communication. On rare occasions I discovered psychics changing information to accommodate their own personal beliefs.

Symbols and pictures have to be converted to language, creating additional possibilities for error. Imagine describing a television set or an airplane to a jungle native who has never experienced it for himself, and expecting him to relay your message to his tribe. What would be the feedback from his people?

Although we have been told that the psychic sensitive is not reading your mind, the fact is that your thoughts CAN interfere with the communication, so it is essential to stay neutral and accepting during a session.

It is also preferable to go alone. Although some are not distracted, there were times when the readings on my wife and me were confused, resulting in her sprained ankle being attributed to me and my new business attributed to her. Best to avoid these risks.

Experienced hypnotists say a person who does not want to be hypnotized cannot be. If you go to a psychic sensitive to challenge him to read on you, he will usually not be able to do so. Even taking along a skeptical friend can prevent the success of a reading. You can argue that a skilled person should be able to use that skill under any circumstances, but in this instance your argument has no validity. What is happening is what's so and must come as it comes through the person you consult if you want to tap this source of knowledge.

In considering the phenomenon of spiritual healing, here again no one seems to know how it occurs. What really counts is that it CAN happen and it CAN work. But, once again, challenging the situation can prevent healing. So if it works for you, be grateful.

To take the position that this body of knowledge does not exist or is not available to us is like sitting in a room where the silence proves there are no radio waves. You would be correct in thinking this until a teenager comes through playing a transistor radio.

In the same sense, it is not necessary to know how it works to use it. Western man's style of thinking has been concerned more with causality than the actual happening. It is questionable whether we shall ever really understand the cause of these phenomena nor is it important. What is essential is that we realize that each event is unique and individual, appreciating it for what it is.

We are travelling through space on a space ship at the rate of hundreds of thousands of miles per second. The ship is called Earth. We must remember that at any given moment we are at a point in time and space. This is what we may call our Here-Now, each of us having only one Here-Now which is gone in an instant. Anything we think or do is really only valid Here-Now, not forever after. Getting information from any of the aforementioned sources must be recognized as only valid at the time. After all, we can only be given what we can comprehend. There are limitations to the knowledge available to us because we are not allowed to have "tomorrow's knowledge with today's wisdom." Learning brings growth, and growth means change.

Though many have been unaware of these relationships, each person has spirit guides available to help him. Perhaps we should become aware of this special relationship and concentrate on contacting them directly with our own tuning sets. Meditation is an excellent way to relax into a receptive level.

Considering that we are still ignorant of the nature of electricity, it is small wonder that we have difficulty in discovering how psychic sensitives operate. The first requirement is to forget about HOW it is working and deal with WHAT is happening. Each sensitive is a unique individual, able to handle the information he gets from the other side with only the skills he has.

I wish you well on your own discoveries. We have before us exciting breakthroughs in our joint quest for the nature of our journey, the meaning of our existence.

Peter Boulton

Suggested Reading
For Psychical Research

General (Elementary)

Anspacher, Louis K.—CHALLENGE OF THE UNKNOWN

Eddy, Sherwood—YOU WILL SURVIVE AFTER DEATH

Fodor, Nandor—ENCYCLOPEDIA OF PSYCHIC SCIENCE

Hart, Hornell—THE ENIGMA OF SURVIVAL

Heywood, Rosalind—BEYOND THE REACH OF SENSE

Lester, Reginald—IN SEARCH OF THE HEREAFTER

Montgomery, Ruth—A SEARCH FOR THE TRUTH

Smith, Alson J.—IMMORTALITY: THE SCIENTIFIC EVIDENCE

Spraggett, Allen—THE UNEXPLAINED

Stearn, Jess—DOOR TO THE FUTURE

General (Advanced)

Broad, C. D.—LECTURES ON PSYCHICAL RESEARCH

Ducasse, C. J.—THE BELIEF IN A LIFE AFTER DEATH

131

Johnson, Raynor C.—THE IMPRISONED SPLENDOUR

Murphy, Gardner—THE CHALLENGE OF PSYCHICAL RESEARCH

Myers, Frederic W. H.—HUMAN PERSONALITY AND ITS SURVIVAL OF BODILY DEATH

Extra-Sensory Perception

Gudas, Fabian J.—EXTRASENSORY PERCEPTION

Rhine, J. B.—REACH OF THE MIND

Apparitions

Fodor, Nandor—THE HAUNTED MIND

Tyrrell, G. N. M.—APPARITIONS

Mediumship

Cummins, Geraldine—THE ROAD TO IMMORTALITY

Garrett, Eileen—MANY VOICES

Sherwood, Jane—THE COUNTRY BEYOND

Sherwood, Jane—POST-MORTEM JOURNAL

White, Stewart E.—THE UNOBSTRUCTED UNIVERSE

Spiritual Healing

Hutton, J. Bernard—HEALING HANDS

Lester, Reginald—TOWARDS THE HEREAFTER

Miscellaneous

Bendit, Phoebe and Laurence—THE PSYCHIC SENSE

Crookall, Robert—THE SUPREME ADVENTURE

Ford, Arthur—NOTHING SO STRANGE

Flew, Anthony—BODY, MIND AND DEATH

Harlow, S. Ralph—A LIFE AFTER DEATH

Lamont, Corliss—THE ILLUSION OF IMMORTALITY

Pike, James A.—THE OTHER SIDE

Pollack, J. H.—CROISET, THE CLAIRVOYANT

Rhine, Louisa E.—HIDDEN CHANNELS OF THE MIND

Sugrue, Thomas—THERE IS A RIVER

Weatherhead, Leslie D.—PSYCHOLOGY, RELIGION AND
    HEALING

Reincarnation

Bernstein, Morey—THE SEARCH FOR BRIDEY MURPHY

Cerminara, Gina—MANY MANSIONS

Kelsey & Grant—MANY LIFETIMES

Montgomery, Ruth—HERE AND HEREAFTER

Stearn, Jess—THE SLEEPING PROPHET

Stevenson, Ian—TWENTY CASES SUGGESTIVE
    OF REINCARNATION

Walker, E. D.—REINCARNATION